To n
ric

HISTORY OF CHESTERFIELD

Volume 2 Part 2

S.W. view of Chesterfield 1812 (by Pickering)

History of

CHESTERFIELD

VOLUME 2 PART 2

Restoration and Georgian Chesterfield

By J.M. Bestall and
D.V. Fowkes

BOROUGH OF CHESTERFIELD
1984

Published by Chesterfield Borough Council

First published 1984

ISBN 0 9510053 0 8

Set in 10/11pt Times New Roman
Produced by Alan Sutton Publishing, Gloucester
Printed in Great Britain

PREFACE

This brief sketch of the history of Chesterfield between 1660 and 1830 incorporates the last work on the town by John Bestall and the local history class that was held under his direction in the 1960s and early 1970s. In contrast to the almost complete manuscripts for Volume I and III of the *History of Chesterfield* which were left at the time of his death in 1973, only a series of notes on a variety of topics existed as the basis for Volume II which was to cover the period between the end of the Wars of the Roses and the accession of Victoria. Mr. Bestall had barely started work at all on the earlier part of this period, so this has been researched by Philip Riden from scratch and published as Vol.II part 1.

For some years after 1973 Mr. Bestall's widow, Barbara, and several former members of the local history class, in particular Miss M. Hewitt, Mrs. R. Milward, Mrs. D. Nolan, Mr. F. Slawson, Mr. W. Watkinson, and Mrs N. Webb, continued to work on various aspects of the town's history in this period and their work on the activities of the vestry and the corporation has been incorporated in this work together with a variety of shorter contributions by individuals on the building of the parish workhouse, the rise of Methodism in Chesterfield and the 1744 churchwardens accounts. My main work has been to attempt to weld these various contributions together and to try and fill in some of the inevitable gaps.

Given the origins of this work, it would be wrong to expect it to be the last word on the history of Chesterfield in this period. It is hoped, however, that it provides a continuity of approach and content with Volume III and it would seem appropriate that the last of John Bestall's work on the history of the town should incorporate research by members of his local history class as the fostering of adult education in Chesterfield was one of his abiding interests.

D.V. Fowkes,
Staffordshire Record Office,
December 1983

CONTENTS

ACKNOWLEDGEMENTS

As always, thanks are due to a variety of institutions and individuals who have assisted in the preparation and publication of this volume. Most of the material used is held by the Derbyshire Record Office, Chesterfield Public Library and the Town Clerk's Department at Chesterfield Town Hall, and I am grateful to the staff of each of these for their considerable assistance throughout the work on this volume. I also have to thank the Chesterfield Borough Planning and Estates Officer for redrawing the map of Chesterfield in about 1800 and for permission to reproduce copies of original documents and photographs I am grateful to Chesterfield Borough Council, Chesterfield Public Library, the Derbyshire Record Office and Mr. R. Pashley.

LIST OF ILLUSTRATIONS

LIST OF MAPS

LIST OF TABLES

CHAPTER 1

THE FABRIC OF THE TOWN

Some outside impressions

It is always interesting to open an account of the topography of a town by studying the impressions formed by contemporary visitors. In general terms, in the case of Chesterfield these became less flattering as the period progressed.

One visitor to Chesterfield in 1662 was a Cambridge graduate of twenty-two who became an eminent physician, who attended Charles II in his last illness and who for the last three years of his life was President of the Royal College of Physicians (1705–8). Unfortunately, Edward Browne, son of Sir Thomas Browne, and his companions who set out from Norwich for a tour of the north Midlands met attrociously bad weather as they travelled from Tuxford to Chesterfield at "an alderman's pace",[1] taking seven hours for what he reckoned was sixteen miles but in modern terms is twenty-seven miles. On reaching their inn in Chesterfield at about mid-day, Browne says, "we crawled upstairs to a fire, where in two houres time we had so well dried ourselves without and liquored ourselves within, that we begant to bee so valiant as to think upon a second march". Their inn, which cannot be identified but was probably The Angel at the top of the Market Place or The Falcon on Low Pavement, was "noted for good drinke and a shovel borde table". That day a number of "Darbisher blades" had been invited there before setting out on their return journey to Bakewell, and Browne thought it would be an advantage to travel with them through "this strange mountainous, misty, morish, rocky, wild country". Only after they had drunk well were the Bakewell men persuaded to accept these strangers whose swords and pistols they viewed with disfavour. The rain had not abated and the flooded roads up and down hills of unfamiliar steepness made the ride to Bakewell a terrifying experience for Browne who lost one of his companions on the way. Because of this chance meeting with local men and the shortness of his stay, Browne left few descriptive comments on Chesterfield relative to Bakewell but it is appropriate that what he did say should centre on a public house, as the presence of some sixty-nine inns, taverns and alehouses[2] to serve a population of perhaps 1500 or so could justifiably be claimed to be the outstanding feature of the town.

An eminent visitor to Chesterfield thirty-five years later was the diarist Celia Fiennes[3]. After commenting on coal mines en route from Eckington, she went on to say, "Chesterfield looks so low when you approach it from the adjacent hill, but then you ascend another to it; the Coale pitts and quaraes of stone are all about even just at the town end, and in the town its all built of stone; the church stands in a place of eminency, the town looks well, the Streets good the Market very large, it was Satturday which is their market day and there was a great Market like some little faire, a great deale of corne and all sorts of ware and fowles, there I bought my self a very good fatt white (pullings as they call them) pullets for 6 pence both, and I am sure they were as large and as good as would have cost 18 pence if not 2 shillings apiece in London, so said all my Company; in this town is the best ale in the kingdom generally esteemed". This short account contains several significant points, the most important being the statement that the town was "all built of stone", the only contemporary allusion to building materials. The pre-eminence she gives to the market is predictable. Less predictable is her failure to note the crooked spire: perhaps it was less crooked at this date or perhaps she had sampled a little too much of the town's best ale.

Visiting the town twenty or so years later in the mid 1720s, Daniel Defoe was also generally complimentary[14]. He described it as "a handsome populous town, well built and well-inhabited, notwithstanding it stands at the farthest part of this rocky country; for being on the north west side next to Yorkshire, it enters Scarsdale which is a rich fruitful part of the county, though surrounded with barren moors and mountains for such the name Scarsdale signifies, according to that master of etymologies Mr. Campden. Here is, however, little remarkable in this town but for a free school and a very good market well stored with provisions; for here is little or no manufacture". To Defoe, therefore, it was the market that was again the most conspicuous feature of the town: one is left doubting his geography and he, also, failed to notice the spire.

Sylas Neville[5] visiting in 1781 is much less complimentary than his predecessors. Reaching the town from Sheffield on 26 October, he remarked that ". . . Chesterfield with its inclined spire looks a fine place at a distance, but entering it you see the people poor and the buildings half in ruins. I cannot account for the miserable appearance of many of the poorer sort in these parts except that men live better by agriculture than manufacturing – one tends to preserve health, the other to destroy it. Many of the children are

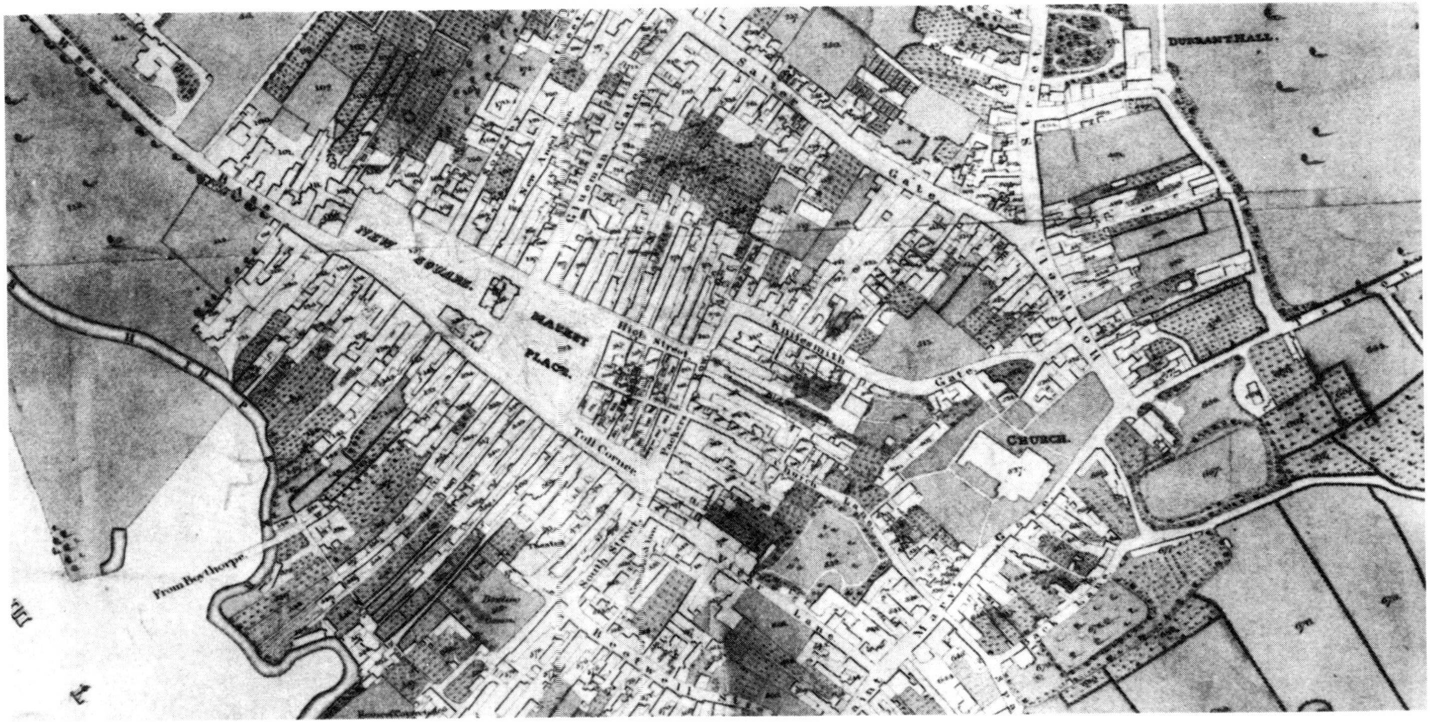

Part of the 1826 poor rate assessment map of Chesterfield showing the centre of the town.

almost naked". One suspects from the latter remarks that Neville had an axe to grind, but the burgeoning population and the infilling of the town centre by the overcrowded yards may well have begun to change the basic character of the town.

Viscount Torrington[6] found little to comment on apart from ". . . the steeple stands most curiously awry" and ". . . the market place is spacious" when he passed through in 1789, which brings us to the generally unflattering descriptions of the early nineteenth century writers. The Rev. D.P. Davies writing in 1811[7] remarked that "Chesterfield is not a place of great trade, nor is there any considerable manufacture carried on in it", but he mentioned with favour Carr's 1787 Town Hall in the Market Place, and the Assembly Rooms at the Castle Inn. This brings us to Richard Phillips and his description of the town in 1828[8] as "dull" and "worn out" which aptly sums up the gloomier accounts of outside observers of the town in the later years of the period.

It is obviously not possible to draw too many conclusions from these accounts of what were clearly fleeting impressions, but it is significant that all the visitors realised the importance of the market to the town, and also the failure of the town to share in the general growth of the industrial revolution period, a fact that was clearly a black mark against it to all of the later observers. It is hard not to conclude also that there was some general deterioration in the fabric of the town with the increasing population and steady infilling of the central area. Against this one cannot help thinking that the views of these 19th century writers may well have been coloured somewhat by the failure to find what they expected of an enterprising town in the opening decades of the 19th century: at the time Phillips was describing it as "dull" and "worn out", pioneer moves were being made towards the supply of piped water and the provision of gas lighting.

Morphology and buildings

The Georgian town some of our travellers were visiting would not have been unfamiliar to a medieval time traveller in several respects. In particular, the street pattern had changed little over the centuries (see Fig.1). The first new street to be formed in the central area was Soresby Street which was created in the opening decade of the 19th century, but Cavendish Street and Burlington Street belong to the early Victorian period. Similarly, the built-up area of the town had not increased significantly. Even within the 298½ acres of the borough there remained plenty of open space: on West Bars beyond New Square, on Saltergate beyond Angel Yard, and on Newbold Road, as well as the Durrant Hall estate, emphasising further the degree to which development was crammed into the medieval core. The long medieval burgage plots stretching down to the Hipper from Low Pavement and Beetwell Street, and between the Market Place and Saltergate, continued to be a dominant feature of the morphology.

The legacy of buildings obviously from this period – a period in which there must have have been a great deal of rebuilding if Celia Fiennes' description was accurate – is not great, particularly from the period before 1800. The Terrace on Saltergate is perhaps the most apparent example of Georgian architecture in the town, together with the "Georgian House" on once fashionable St. Mary's Gate. There is also the pedimented "Secker's House" in the north west corner of New Square. Of the ecclesiastical buildings, the Elder Yard Chapel and the Rose Hill Independent Chapel of 1821 survive, along with the much-altered Saltergate Methodist Chapel of 1795. What would have been the great industrial monument to the period – the silk mill off Beetwell Street – has gone, together with the old council house on the Bowling Green, the parish workhouse, the theatre and Carr's Town Hall of 1787 on the north side of the Market Place. Just outside of the ancient borough boundary in what was part of Brampton, the "Cannon Mill", traditionally attributed to 1815, and the early iron-framed building at the junction of Furnace Lane and Wheatbridge Road, serve to remind us of the heyday of Ebenezer Smith's ironworks.

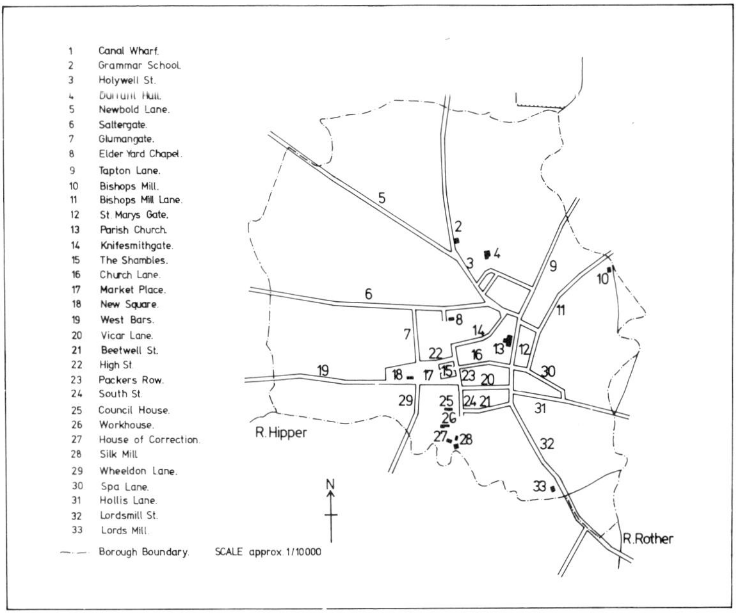

Fig.1 Chesterfield in about 1800

Population

The bare statistics of population figures between 1660 and 1830 reveal a great deal about the development of the town over this period. Official statistics are not, of course, available until 1801 so the first truly reliable figure we have is the population of 4267 in that year. However, there are certain statistics available prior to 1801 that provide us with some idea of the order of population at various dates and consequently some pointers to the chronology and rate of development of the town over this period (see Tables 1 and 2).

Table 1 Aggregative totals from Chesterfield parish registers 1721–1800

	Baptisms	Burials	
1721–1740	1943	1676	conjectural population of c.2500
1741–1760	1894	1780	
1761–1780	2389	2043	
1781–1800	4027	2636	

Based on a count carried out by members of Mr. Bestall's local history class.

Table 2 Summary of the population statistics for Chesterfield 1662–1831

Source	*Date*	*Houses*	*Males*	*Females*	*Total*	*Persons per house*
Hearth tax	1664	315	households		1500	
Eden	1783	777			3335	4.29
Pilkington	1788	801			3626	4.39
Eden	1791	866	1929		3987	4.60
Census	1801	920	2025	2338	4267	4.76
Census	1811	979	2345	2451	4476	4.71
Census	1821	1079	2665	2732	5077	4.84
Census	1831	1264		3110	5775	4.78

There are, of course, many problems involved in the interpretation of the Hearth Tax returns of the mid seventeenth century, but in 1662 the township of Chesterfield appears to have had some 315 families[9] which would seem to indicate a population of around 1500 at this time. The figure of 3500 given in the so-called "Compton Census"[10] is impossible to interpret as we do not know which people are included (i.e. just adult males, all adults or total inhabitants) nor how much of the parish, as distinct from the township, was included[11]. Unofficial censuses by Eden in 1783[12], by Pilkington in 1788[12], and by Eden again in 1791[14], show the population to have reached the mid 3000s by the 1780s, confirming the period of net increase in the second half of the eighteenth century which aggregative analysis of the parish registers seems to suggest[15]. The same analysis suggests that the population in the first half of the eighteenth century would have been fairly static probably at around the 2000 mark.

As Table 2 shows, the population increased steadily in the opening decades of the nineteenth century with the greatest actual increase between 1821 and 1831 so that between 1801 and 1831 the population had increased by around one-third. This was far from exceptional, however, in a period when population was increasing rapidly almost everywhere, and it is interesting to note that the population of neighbouring Brampton, where much of the development of mineral-based industry took place over this period, increased from 2047 in 1801 to 3574 in 1831, an increase of around three-quarters. The main practical result of the much enhanced population was that more and more people were crammed into the town centre which, as we have seen, was still very much limited to its medieval core. The number of houses increased by almost three-quarters between 1783 and 1831, many of them built in the yards leading off the main thoroughfares and it was these courts that became a byword for overcrowding and insanitary conditions.

An interesting aspect of the population structure is the substantial excess of females over males in the census period, a phenomenon that is not easily explained in a town with only one substantial textile factory, and a hosiery industry that was apparently in decline over this period. Perhaps large numbers of domestic servants in the town's many public houses, town houses and retail establishments is the answer, possibly combined with some outward movement of male labour to the nearby developing industrial areas.

CHAPTER 2

RUNNING THE TOWN

The Borough

Some seventeenth century glimpses

Some of the few glimpses of the activities of the corporation before the late 18th century come in the years immediately following the Restoration. The Corporation Act of 1661, the first of the statutes in the so-called Clarendon Code, was passed by the Cavalier Parliament to ensure that the government of boroughs was in the hands of men well disposed towards the restored monarchy. It required all members of corporations to take the oaths of allegiance and supremacy, to swear that it was unlawful to take arms against the king and to repudiate all obligations based on the Solemn League and Covenant of 1643. Commissioners were appointed in each county to administer these oaths. Their visit to Chesterfield produced a drastic change in the personnel of the corporation.[1] The mayor, Hercules Clay, refused to subscribe to these oaths and was replaced by a conforming alderman, John Allwood. Four other aldermen, William Newton, Thomas Needham, Thomas Forth and Gilbert Heathcote were expelled and the vacancies filled by the appointment of Ralph Ashe, Richard Marchant, Thomas Large, Thomas Pinder and Richard Cadwell as new aldermen. Amongst the brethren Roger Coates, Richard Youle, Robert Stringfellow and Thomas Bretland were replaced by James Milnes, grocer, Edward Needham, Anthony Legate, James Dutton and William Mackson. Seven capital burgesses were then similarly removed, Edward Revell, Humphrey Pettie, Adam Gill, John Stones, George White and Michael Watton for refusing to take the oaths and James Milnes, ironmonger, for failing to attend. Nine new capital burgesses were then appointed to bring the corporation up to full strength, John Marsden, Francis Marples, Thomas Slater, Geoffrey Shaw, John Hosland, Thomas Needham, Francis Gilberthorpe, John Shaw and Hewyn Leatherland. The effect of this act, therefore, was to replace fifteen of the twenty-five members of the corporation by others more sympathetic to the claims of the monarchy and the Anglican church.

Ten years later we find the corporation reviewing both its plate and its customs.[2] In September 1671 Richard Clarke, the vintner who was elected mayor for the first time in 1670, proposed that the corporation should sell its plate in order to buy a mace. An inventory, taken in October, showed that the corporation possessed three or four bowls, a gilt salt with cover and about thirty spoons, weighing together 97½ ounces and valued at £23 19s 5d. The spoons had been received from members of the gilds or trading companies on completion of their apprenticeship. It was decided that the silver should be melted down to make a mace, but another 40 ounces was required to produce a satisfactory result. The silver at 10s. an ounce, with the other costs of production, required a payment of £46 1s 3d from the corporation. The mace thus produced was fifty-four inches long, with its head divided into four compartments, containing a rose, a thistle and portcullis, a harp, and a fleur-de-lis,each crowned and between the initials (CR) of Charles II. The royal arms within the garter appear on the top, and the initials are repeated. It has been pointed out in the standard works on civic heraldry that there are certain errors in the blazonry of the shield on the Chesterfield mace.

In 1675 the corporation found it desirable to regulate the customs which had grown up at the annual mayor-making. After the taking of oaths and the formal installation, the mayor was proclaimed from the market cross and in the main streets, a sermon was preached in the parish church by the vicar, for which he received a fee of £1, and later there was the mayor's feast, for which the corporation allowed the very generous sum of £60. This feast had been open to members of the corporation, the masters of the trade companies and all the common burgesses, but the company had become so large that it was decided that in future the common burgesses could attend only by invitation of the mayor. The four companies of shoemakers, butchers, tailors and smiths were still allowed to attend the feast if they had earlier been present at the mayor's proclamation; failure to attend the proclamation not only excluded them from the feast but also made them liable to a fine of 2s 6d. The traditional monthly feasts were to be continued for members of the corporation only, but the annual allowance of £15 made to the mayor was stopped in 1675.

The expenditure on the mayor's feast does not appear in the accounts of John Ashe and William Dowker, chamberlains to Richard Clarke, mayor of Chesterfield for the year 1678 (see Appendix A). This single year of seventeenth century accounts has survived among the Pashley papers[3] and provides the only detailed view of the finances of the Corporation in the seventeenth century.

From the previous chamberlain Francis Holdsworth, they received from the corporation stock £61 10s 9d and from the Godfrey Foljambe bequest (Brackenfield annuity and Ashover rents) £39 6s 8d. This income of roughly £100 was supplemented by all the rents from corporation property, interest on other charity monies, notably the earl of Shrewsbury's, and occasional payments, such as the burgess fine of 10s from William Beatson or the spoon money (12s) paid by John Osland, producing a total income of almost £170. Rents ranged from 2s 6d to £7 10s 0d and were paid by only fourteen people for four houses, including one called Gatehouse, which has not yet been identified, four shops, including three under the Market Hall and one in the butchery, and various pieces of land including Cockpit Yard, Boythorpe Closes, the Tenters and the Horse Mill. These payments at least demonstrate the corporation's role as a property owner.

The allowances and disbursements were more varied in character. They included payments to the mayor, such as his allowance of £10 and his expenses for going to the assizes or to Welbeck, to the town clerk for his salary of £6 and various expenses, and to the clerk of the peace £2 when the mayor took the prescribed oaths at Quarter Sessions. The only expenditure directly concerned with the public good was the series of payments made to the overseers of Chesterfield and those of the townships of the old parish. These payments were derived from the income of lands acquired though the bequests of Godfrey Foljambe and formed a supplement to the money raised from the poor rate in these places. The corporation had to pay hearth tax for the council house and a few small rents including 10s for the town hall, which remained, of course, a manorial rather than borough institution well into the nineteenth century. The continuing subordination to the Cavendishes can also be seen reflected in the sending of "veale and a mutton" to Welbeck, and veal to Hardwick, at a cost respectively of £2 5s 0d and £1 6s 8d, a custom which persisted for long after this date. Other miscellaneous payments include £5 4s 0d to Widow Greaves for bread, presumably her charges for baking bread for distribution to the poor throughout the year under the terms of certain charities; 15s 0d to Anthony Woodward for ringing the church bells on some unspecified occasion; £1 7s 0d to Job Brundley, a bookseller, for a new prayer book and the latest volume of the acts of parliament; £1 for a sermon and another £5 for unknown services to Mr. Coope the vicar; and some small expenses such as 1s 6d for a new lock and band for the bowling green door and 6s 8d to James Lambert for the dyehouse. The total expenditure amounted to £101 17s 2d and with arrears, including the mayor's rent for Cockpit Yard, coming to £6 3s 0d, the chamberlains retained just over £60, of which £57 12s 0d was passed on to their successors.

From this isolated set of accounts showing the state of the borough finances at this date, only one or two rather obvious comments can be made. There is firstly the small scale of the corporation's financial activities which, in turn reflects the continuing small scale of its activities generally, with the manor and parish still carrying out the majority of the town's local government functions: even its property was, in fact, largely Foljambe charity property. Secondly, and closely related to the last point, is the nature of the corporation, in particular the extent to which it appears as a private rather than a public corporate body, and, as such, making little contribution to the well-being of the town.

Yet another incident demonstrating the impotence of the corporation in relation to the lord of the manor occurred in 1688[4]. In July of that year, the mayor, Richard Youle, had to report to the Duke of Newcastle at Welbeck that the town clerk of Chesterfield, William Champernoun, had died and that in accordance with the town's charters Ralph Adderley had been chosen. The appointment required royal approval and it is interesting that this was not sought directly by the mayor but through the medium of the lord of the manor. Newcastle commended their choice saying of Adderley, "he is my servant and a very loyal man and lives in the towne". Another statement from the same incident sheds further light on the contemporary view of the status of the borough, with Newcastle stating ". . . the towne is mine and I am very much beholding to the Corporation, but they send noe parliament men but may have their votes as freeholders for the county". Adderley was, in fact, appointed town clerk, an office he filled until his death in 1705.

The corporation in the late eighteenth and early nineteenth centuries

It is not until 1783 that systematically kept records of the corporation become available[5]. It is interesting to speculate whether a minute of 28 September 1789 ordering that "all the writings belonging to the Corporation in whosoever's custody be immediately deposited in the chest for the purpose of enabling the committee to inspect the same" was at all responsible for minutes being kept, albeit incompletely, from this date. Any previous minutes, proceedings or order books have been lost. By pure coincidence, the vestry minutes also survive from 1782, so from this date onwards it is possible to gain an insight into the detailed working of the two bodies for the first time. It has to be said from the outset that by twentieth century standards neither body was overwhelmed with business and much of what business there was concerned merely the appointment of officials, the election of

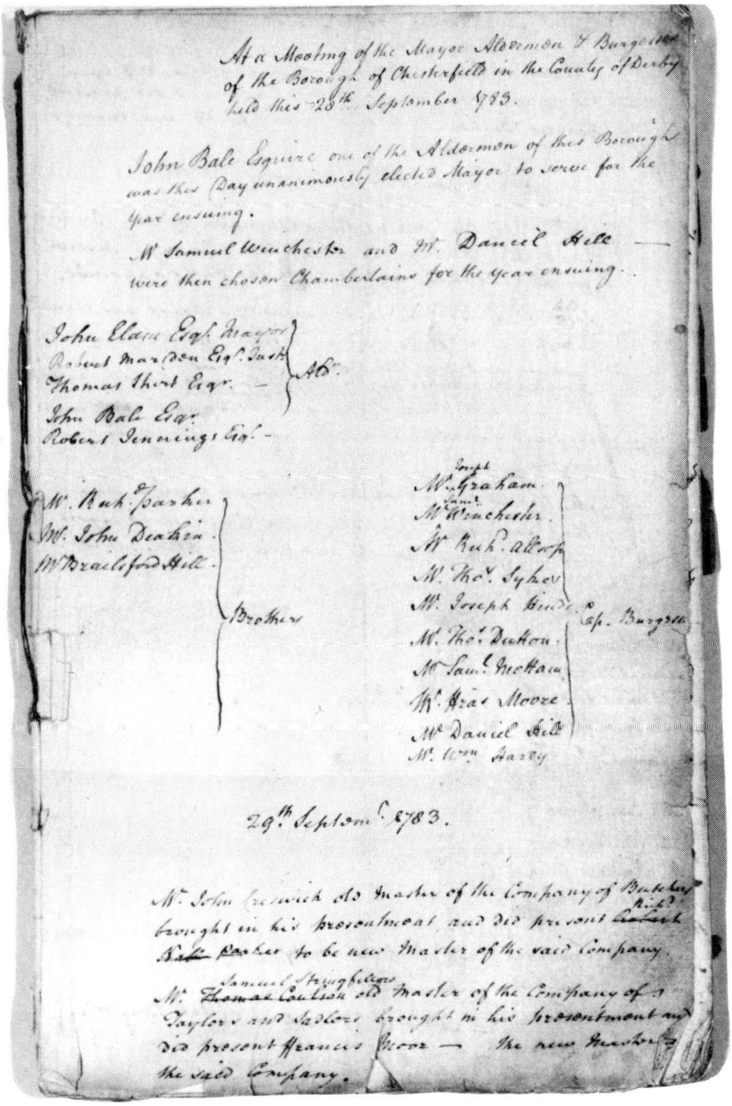

At a Meeting of the Mayor Aldermen & Burgesses of the Borough of Chesterfield in the County of Derby held this 28th September 1783.

John Bale Esquire one of the Aldermen of this Borough was this Day unanimously elected Mayor to serve for the Year ensuing.

Mr Samuel Winchester and Mr Daniel Hill — were then chosen Chamberlains for the Year ensuing.

John Elam Esqr Mayor
Robert Marsden Esqr Justice
Thomas Thirst Esqr — } Aldn
John Bale Esqr
Robert Jennings Esqr —

Mr Richd Parker
Mr John Deakin } Brothers
Mr Brailsford Hill

Mr Joseph Graham
Mr Saml Winchester
Mr Richd Allsop
Mr Thos Sykes
Mr Joseph Hinde } Cap. Burgesses
Mr Thos Dutton
Mr Saml Mottram
Mr Fras Moore
Mr Daniel Hill
Mr Wm Harvey

29th Septemr 1783.

Mr John Creswick old Master of the Company of Butchers brought in his presentment and did present Richd Parker to be new Master of the said Company.

Mr ~~Thomas Coulson~~ Samuel Stringfellow old Master of the Company of Taylors and Sadlers brought in his presentment and did present Francis Moore — the new Master of the said Company.

Opening page of the first surviving minute book of Chesterfield Borough Council, 28 September 1783 burgesses, the preparation of loyal addresses to the crown and the like. Many of the proceedings are therefore repetitive and devoid of any great interest. It is perhaps a significant commentary on the activities of the unreformed corporation that what would have been the most significant event in the last fifty years of its existence did not take place. This was the abortive atempt in 1794–5 to obtain a separate borough quarter sessions for the town as part of the application for a new charter. Chesterfield had always been exceptional as a borough without the administration of justice in its own hands within its boundaries.

The corporation had no fixed meeting place but most meetings took place at the Council House on the Bowling Green built in 1620 and increasingly inaccurately referred to as the "New House" even in the 1780s. Occasionally meetings were held in public houses – The Commercial Inn and the Angel Inn are referred to – and sometimes in the town clerk's office in the Wallers' days. Significantly there is only one reference to a meeting in the Town Hall (4 June 1800) which was normally used by the Manor Court and the county magistrates. Indeed, perhaps not surprisingly, the building of the new Town Hall in 1787–8 passes by without even an oblique reference.

Present-day councillors would be amazed at the infrequency of meetings in the latter stages of the unreformed corporation. The only meetings that invariably took place were the 24 June (feast of St John the Baptist) and 28 or 29 September (Michaelmas) meetings. At the June meeting the mayor for the forthcoming year was nominated and at the September meeting he was elected. In years like 1793 and 1797, little else happened, at least that was recorded, although even in these uneventful years the Michaelmas meeting normally lasted for two or three days. Clearly the good burgesses concentrated their minds in autumn. Mayors could not serve in successive years but there was nothing to stop them serving alternate years. Thomas Dutton, for example, was mayor eight times between 1783 and 1805 as Table 3 shows. In the year following his mayoralty, he was traditionally elected the borough's justice of the peace, to serve on the bench with the mayor for the time being.

Very typically therefore, we find that the only recorded event in the minutes of the meeting of the corporation of 28 September 1783, the first meeting for which minutes have survived, was the election of John Bale as mayor and Samuel Winchester and Daniel Hill as chamberlains. The recital of the aldermen (John Elam, mayor, Robert Marsden, Thomas Shirt, John Bale, Robert Jennings), brothers (Richard Parker, John Deakin, Brailsford Hill) and capital burgesses (Joseph Graham, Samuel Winchester, Richard Allsopp, Thomas Sykes, Joseph Hinde, Thomas Dutton, Samuel Mettam, Francis Moore, Daniel Hill, William Hardy)

Table 3

Mayors referred to in the surviving borough minutes 1782–1834

1782–3	John Elam	1801–2	John Bower
1783–4	John Bale	1802–3	Thomas Dutton
1784–5	John Elam	1803–4	John Bower
1785–6	Thomas Dutton	1804–5	John Elam
1786–7	John Bale	1805–6	Thomas Dutton
1787–8	Thomas Dutton	1818–9	Samuel Dutton
1788–9	Mark Hewitt	1819–20	Joseph Graham
1789–90	John Bale	1820–1	Samuel Dutton
1790–1	Thomas Dutton	1821–2	John Elam
1791–2	John Bradley	1822–3	John Mugliston
1792–3	Thomas Dutton	1823–4	Gilbert Crompton
1793–4	John Elam	1824–5	Samuel Dutton
1794–5	Job Bradley	1825–6	John Elam
1795–6	John Elam	1826–7	George Fletcher
1796–7	John Bower	1827–8	John Mugliston
1797–8	Thomas Dutton	1828–9	Thomas Wilcockson
1798–9	John Bower	1829–30	William Batteson
1799–00	John Saxton	1830–1	Samuel Dutton
1800–1	Thomas Dutton	1831–2	John Mugliston
		1832–3	William Batteson
		1833–4	Samuel Dutton

present, completed the record of that meeting. The corporation in these years was predictably dominated by the commercial element: grocers, innkeepers, manufacturers and merchants. A relatively small group of names recur time and again: the local landed interests are normally conspicuous by their absence. For some strange reason the meeting continued into the following day when John Creswick the "old master" of the Company of Butchers presented his successor Richard Parker as the new master: similarly Samuel Stringfellow, master of the Company of Tailors and Sadlers presented his successor Francis Moore, and Adam Barber, "old master" of the Smiths and Braziers Company his successor Francis Barber. The trade companies were to some extent the lineal descendants of the medieval guilds and the outmoded custom of presenting their new masters had typically survived the centuries. John Bale's predecessor mayor, John Elam, was then sworn justice of the peace for the coming year and Francis Moore was admitted and sworn as a common burgess. It may seem tedious to recite these proceedings in full, but they serve to demonstrate both the survival of archaic customs and the preoccupation with mundane appointments and pure formalities at many of the meetings. An unexpected ingredient was injected into the proceedings at the 1789 mayor-making meeting when John Deakin refused to serve and had to be replaced by John Bale: Deakin was fined for his refusal.

The next meeting on 23 October 1783 demonstrated the type of reason for which an extra meeting might be called. The sole purpose of this meeting, attended by the mayor, the borough's J.P's, three other aldermen and ten capital burgesses, was to "consider and determine" whether the corporation should, or should not, sign the certificate of Thomas Allwood, a grocer formerly of Chesterfield, who was a bankrupt and a debtor to the corporation in the sum of £338 10s 5d. It was decided by a majority of nine to six that the certificate should be signed (i.e. Allwood declared a bankrupt) and this concluded the meeting. At this time, Richard Slater, a local attorney was clerk to the corporation, a position he retained until 1791 when he was replaced by another Chesterfield attorney Robert Waller, beginning an association with the Waller family that was to last until 1857. Robert Waller was clerk until 12 June 1818 when he was replaced by his son William who died in harness in 1857.

It was the following meeting on 5 March 1784 that introduces us to the corporation's main concern at this time, apart from the appointments and ceremonial, namely the administration of corporation property, both that which it owned in fee simple and the charity estates of which it was the trustee. The two estates were to all intents and purposes treated as one and it was this practice that led to a great deal of trouble in the late 1820s. At this meeting, the property concerned was "closes, lands and premises" on Newbold Lane formerly in the possession of Robert Clarke and Hugh Crofts. They were leased to Richard Allsopp for 21 years at an annual rent of £8 12s 0d. At the same meeting the Town Clerk was ordered to write to the clerk of the Rotherham-Mansfield Turnpike Trust demanding the payment of a reasonable sum of money in compensation for three roods of land taken out of the corporation's (in fact, charities') farm at Barlborough to widen the turnpike road. The closes at Newbold referred to were, in fact, four closes belonging to Large's Charity, which had a substantial land endowment in Chesterfield itself, Newbold, Hasland, Calow and Boythorpe, whilst the land at Barlborough was part of the lands belonging to the Heathcote Charities despite its description as the "corporation's" in the minutes[6]. There were some 42 acres in Barlborough alone and substantial holdings in Unstone, Apperknowle, Tapton, Snitterton, Darley, Matlock and Walton. The total corporation and charities estate was therefore considerable in area and by no means confined to the borough and its immediate environs, and the corporation was therefore involved in the same sort of business as any landlord including the leasing of minerals.

As land in Snitterton was involved, the corporation had various encounters with the laws and customs of the lead mining area of the Low Peak.

In their business dealings, the members of the corporation hardly behaved in a way that would find favour today. Several members of the corporation were tenants of corporation or charity property and therefore their own landlord. Nothing was put out to tender, wherever possible work being done within the small exclusive circle of the aldermen, brethren and capital burgesses. Aldermen and burgesses awarded each other contracts for surveying, repair work, lease of minerals etc. with gay abandon, so that one is left gain with the impression of a tight little group still basically concerned with furthering their mutual interests, in precisely the same way as the guilds of the medieval period. Thus, when in 1789 it was resolved that a Bowling Green house should be built, the contract for building it was awarded to Samuel Mettam, one of the capital burgesses: similarly, it was decided in the same year that the stable and outbuilding at Newbold in the possession of Richard Allsopp should be pulled down and rebuilt in accordance with a plan by Francis Moore and Samuel Mettam, both capital burgesses. Moore was also to carry out the carpenter's work. In the same year an estates committee was effectively formed with Thomas Dutton, Job Bradley and Samuel Mettam being appointed as a standing committee to "look over and inspect all the buildings and premises belong to the corporation and to report their condition quarterly".

In 1790–1 there was an extraordinary row with the vestry regarding the parish workhouse in South Place which was adminis tered by the vestry through the overseers of the poor but which the corporation claimed as its property as it was built on corporation land. The row started at the meeting of 1 April 1790 when the chamberlain gave notice to the overseers and the following Tuesday's vestry meeting that the rent for the workhouse would be raised to £5 per annum and that if the increased sum was not paid, a notice to quit would be served at Michaelmas. The overseers did not comply and the notice was served but eventually a compromise was being sought in June 1791 with the vestry proposing a rent of 2 guineas per annum. The vestry of 31 October 1791 again rejected the corporation's terms, however, and the squabble was not resolved until 2 November at a joint meeting of "Town and Corporation" at the Falcon Inn by which it was agreed that the vestry took a 99 year lease of the workhouse at 2 guineas per annum, a lease that still survives among the corporation's archives[7]. A further part of the compromise was that the corporation be allowed to meet at the workhouse to distribute charity money.

This episode sheds a remarkable light on the relationship

between corporation and vestry. There was invariably, and indeed inevitably, a great deal of cross-membership between the two bodies, including the mayor, who regularly attended vestry meetings, and almost all of the corporation committee chosen to negotiate the settlement were also members of the vestry. However, the degree of cross-membership was nothing like as marked as that between the corporation and the manor court at this date when the jury of the manor court tended to consist almost exclusively of leading aldermen and burgesses. It was probably the presence of a substantial "independent" element among the members of the vestry that caused the dispute to develop and continue. It nevertheless seems an apt reflection on the haphazard conduct of affairs that nobody really did seem to know who did own the workhouse and it is not clear whether any rent at all had been paid to the corporation before 1791. Because of the corporation's lack of any day-to-day role in the running of the town's affairs and services, and perhaps because of the degree of cross membership between the four bodies involved in governing the town, examples of minor power struggles of this type are rare in these later years of the unreformed borough: this is indeed the only example of the corporation trying to impose its authority on the "town".

Most of the other estate matters that crop up in the years up to 1834 are routine. The theatre, another building that actually belonged to the corporation, located at this time in Theatre Yard, just below Low Pavement, appears in the minutes with increasing regularity after 1825. A year later the corporation baths on Derby Road were built at a cost of £393 1s 0d. In the years 1825–7 there was a recurring problem regarding alleged damage by ore buddlers on the farm at Snitterton and Matlock which was part of the charity estate. They were said to have exceeded the powers authorised by the lead mining customs of Wirksworth Wapentake: the Barmaster did not agree. Industrial pollution of another kind occurred in Chesterfield itself with the erection of a flax-dressing shop adjacent to Workhouse Meadow. At the end of the 1820s the matter of the Grammar School estates came to a head, with the corporation charged with a debt of £719 5s 7d on the school estates following the report of the Commissioners Enquiring into Charities.

So much for the estate matters that took up so much of the corporation's time. Finally what may be described as the ceremonial aspects of corporation life – the mayor's Rent Day Feast, the members' ceremonial attire and the like – received a considerable amount of attention. As has been seen from the few surviving seventeenth century accounts, the corporation's only regular source of income was from the rents received from its properties, the beneficiaries of parish rates being the vestry and, of course, the county of the county rate. A sizeable sum of money was nevertheless allocated annually for the Midsummer Feast Day and the Rent Feast Day. In 1786, because of the corporation raising a loan of £170, the mayor was limited to £15 for his feast, but in 1787 this was increased to £20, and in 1789 to £25. During the Napoleonic Wars the feasts were suspended as in 1798 £100 was subscribed by the corporation to the government for defraying the expenses of the French War. A further order suspending feasts was made in 1801. By 1823, however, the allowance to the mayor and burgesses for the Rent Day Feast had been increased to £60–70. With the school debt looming on the horizon however, economy measures were soon in hand again: in 1827 future mayors' feasts were to be limited to private feasts and in 1830 the Rent Day dinner was abandoned.

Chesterfield's eighteenth century councillors clearly wore distinctive regalia. In 1785 each member was ordered to take care of his own gown, and the annual sum of £1 paid to Thomas Coulson for the care of the gowns was to cease. In 1788 a further resolution declared that if any member spoilt or lost his gown, he should provide a new one. At a meeting on 25 June 1791, new gowns were ordered for the mayor, justice and town clerk, but the trimmings on the gowns of the brothers and common councillors were to be altered from red to a more sombre black.

The three corporation pews in the parish church also received their fair share of attention as they had consistently done over the centuries. In 1784 officers of the excise were ordered not to sit in the "burgess seat" in the church and in 1785 it was "divided by a partition" so that no one else could make use of it. In 1790 the Rev. Bossley, on whose sermons several comments were passed and minuted over the years, was asked to make use of his seat or give it up. In 1821 prayer books were supplied in the corporation pews, the beadle being allowed 5s per annum for his trouble in placing them during the week, and in 1822 the pews were "new-lined", specimens of crimson cloth or serge being produced at the Feast Day in order to be selected. Finally, in 1824 twelve quarto bibles were purchased and placed in the corporation pews.

The story of the reform of the borough following the Municipal Corporations Act of 1835 belongs to Volume III of this history, but it can be seen from the foregoing that even by the standards of the late eighteenth century the corporation as constituted was an anachronism playing only a minimal role in the everyday life of the town and devoid of any form of popular basis. Ownership of ancient burgage plots continued to be the qualification for membership and therefore for voting rights: its property provided its only revenue and the administration of this property remained its chief practical concern. Clearly in a burgeoning early nineteenth century market town, with pretentions to be an industrial town, change was needed.

The role of the county administration in the government of Chesterfield

As was mentioned earlier, in 1794 the borough had attempted to obtain a separate quarter sessions for the town which would have been a very significant step forwards in increasing its functions and powers, both legal and administrative, virtually rendering it independent of the county authority. This was not to be however, so the county quarter sessions continued to be responsible for the administration of justice and for several important administrative matters, notably overall supervision of the vestry for the operation of the poor and highway laws. The county administration therefore, represented a fourth element in the government of the borough adding to the complexities of the picture. Many licencing matters in the town remained the responsibility of the county authorities: alehouses, nonconformist places of worship, and by the eighteenth century a host of less well-known matters such as free masons, printing presses and theatres, as central government gave more and more work to quarter sessions. Among the old county records therefore, there is a great deal of source material relating to Chesterfield, use of which has been made throughout this volume.

A recognisable county administration by the justices of the peace through the court of quarter sessions dates in practice from the Statute of Labourers of 1555 which gave the justices overall supervision of the implementation of the provisions of that act which was to remain the basis of highway legislation until 1835. This administrative role was greatly boosted by similar responsibilities in relation to the Poor Laws of 1598 and 1601, and a slightly later act of 1609 which had an almost immediate impact on the town. The Derbyshire justices acted very quickly in response to this act which enabled the justices to provide houses of correction for setting to work vagrants and other categories of poor who presented problems to the authorities. By 1613 steps were being taken to acquire a site in Chesterfield. The deeds for the "Cockpit Property", as it was known, survive among the records of the Town Clerk's Department[8]. The earliest deed dates from 12 October 1612 when Sir Thomas Foljambe agreed to convey to Godfrey Webster the elder and Martin Bretland, tanners, "all that messuage or tenement with all houses, buildings, cockpitt, orchard and garden belonging in Chesterfield now in the occupation of Godfrey Cade butcher". Less than a year later (17 May 1613) a deed of declaration by Lady Anne Foljambe, widow of Sir Thomas, and Sir John Molineux declared that the property would be conveyed to Webster's and Boller's use provided that "they cause to be conveyed so much of the said messuage etc. as shall be required to build a house of correction as shall be thought fit by Sir

John Molineux and two other justices". In the following year (29 April 1614) Webster and Boller conveyed to several justices (William, Lord Cavendish, of Hardwick, Sir Francis Leake of Sutton Scarsdale, Sir John Molineux of Teversal, Sir George Manners of Haddon and Sir Peter Frecheville of Staveley) sufficient of the property to build the house of correction namely "all that part or parcel of a close of meadow or pasture called Cockpitt Yard or Cockpitt Close 1½ roods" on the condition that on the parcel there should be built "one house of correction having a convenient backside and other easements thereto adjoining for the punishment and setting to work of all such idle, wandering and other disordered persons as shall be apprehended within the hundreds of Scarsdale and High Peak". The residue of the property was subsequently acquired by the corporation hence the presence of the deeds among the borough archives. In a deed of 26 September 1616 the boundaries of the house of correction are given as the River Hipper to the south and "Ratton Rowe" (Beetwell Street) to the north, indicating its position on the periphery of the built-up area.

The Civil War period must have imposed an exceptional strain both upon the house and its master, for during the Commonwealth John Whittaker petitioned the justices[9]. He complained that despite an earlier order of Quarter Sessions, the high constables of Scarsdale and High Peak had not paid him his authorised wages and had failed to maintain the master's house properly. As a result of this neglect and the losses he suffered in the house of correction at the beginning of the war, Whittaker found himself "much impoverished and not well able to subsist".

The house of correction continued to supplement the county gaol as a place where vagrants and minor offenders could be interned until well into the nineteenth century and it is an interesting and apt reflection on attitudes to the poor and the causes of poverty that the seventeenth century poor laws should have incorporated such a punitive element.

Returning to the more general work of the justices, it was customary for the Derbyshire Sessions to be held each year twice at Derby, in the spring and autumn, at Chesterfield in January, and at Bakewell (or occasionally Wirksworth) in July. The Derbyshire records are unfortunately very fragmentary before 1682 when the systematic sessions order books begin, one cause of loss being this custom of holding the sessions in different centres with the consequent need to transport books and papers around the county.

Apart from several ale-house licencing papers, the pre 1682 loose papers consist largely of depositions made in criminal or poor law cases coming before the court and parish constables' presentments of malefactors, usually people failing to attend

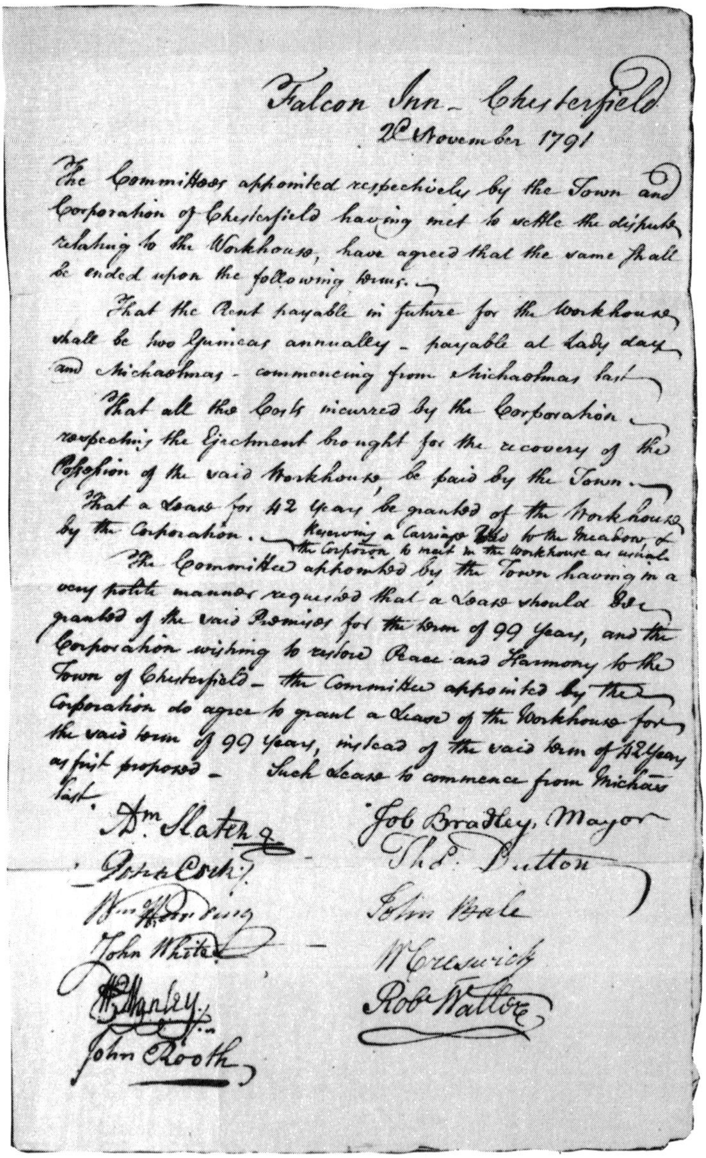

Falcon Inn – Chesterfield
2d November 1791

The Committees appointed respectively by the Town and Corporation of Chesterfield having met to settle the dispute relating to the Workhouse, have agreed that the same shall be ended upon the following terms.—

That the Rent payable in future for the Workhouse shall be two Guineas annually – payable at Lady day and Michaelmas – commencing from Michaelmas last.

That all the Costs incurred by the Corporation respecting the Ejectment brought for the recovery of the Possession of the said Workhouse, be paid by the Town.—

That a Lease for 42 Years be granted of the Workhouse by the Corporation. — Reserving a Carriage [illegible] to the Meadow of the Corporation to meet in the Workhouse as usual.

The Committee appointed by the Town having in a very polite manner requested that a Lease should be granted of the said Premises for the term of 99 Years, and the Corporation wishing to restore Peace and Harmony to the Town of Chesterfield – the Committee appointed by the Corporation do agree to grant a Lease of the Workhouse for the said term of 99 Years, instead of the said term of 42 Years as first proposed – Such Lease to commence from Michaelmas last.

Wm Slater — Job Bradley, Mayor
[illegible] — Thos. Dutton
Wm [illegible] — John Bale
John White — W Creswick
W. Manley — Robt Wallace
John Booth

Agreement between the town and the corporation regarding the payment of rent for the parish workhouse, 2 November 1791

church or people brewing ale without a licence. Like those of most other places in the county, Chesterfield inhabitants crop up from time to time among these depositions. For example a very human story was told by Ellen Croft in her undated examination before one of the local justices, Ralph Clarke[10]. She had "kept company about foure years with George Boler of Brimington whoe att the aforesaid tyme promissed to marrie her"; the previous June when she was a servant of Francis Moore in Chesterfield she met Boler in the house of William Crofts and "then and there the said Boler had the carnall use of her bodie" in the same house, and she was expecting a child in March. Two years earlier when Boler went to Scotland as a trooper in Captain Gabriel Wayne's troop a piece of silver was broken between them which she understood to be "in testimony of a contract . . . of marriage". From Scotland Boler had sent her "divers letters and tokens".

In the later years of the period, the minor offenders coming before the court were dealt with at a fortnightly petty sessions for the borough – the predecessor of the present-day magistrates court – meeting at the town clerk's office[11].

The Vestry

The third body involved in the government of the town was the vestry acting in its civil capacity. Apart from the "suppression of nuisances" which was very much the continued prerogative of the manor court, such public services as there were in the town in this period were largely provided by the vestry. Law and order seemed to occupy a somewhat ambiguous position with both the manor court and the vestry apparently involved in the appointment of the constables.

As with the justices, the administrative functions of the vestry date back to the Tudor period, to the renowned Statute of Labourers once again, which transferred the responsibility for the upkeep of roads from the manor to the previously exclusively ecclesiastical unit of the parish. Unfortunately, particularly in view of Chesterfield's size and importance, the records for studying the work of the vestry are virtually non-existent for much of the period, and when they do surface in 1782 it has to be said that they are a grave disappointment as only the minutes of vestry meetings, often giving only the most summary account of events, have survived. A vast corpus of loose papers, overseers, constables and surveyors accounts, and all the paraphernalia involved in the administration of the laws relating to settlement, bastardy and apprenticeship has disappeared almost without trace, leaving us clutching at straws for the study of several key aspects of the civil administration. Only a few oddments in the Pashley and Blockley collections in the Derbyshire Record Office, the occasional reference in quarter sessions order books and the accounts for building the parish workhouse in 1734 survive to provide any insight into the civil affairs of the vestry before the minutes begin in 1782.

The care of the poor

In 1734–6 there was a major step forward in the provision for the relief of the poor in the town. Under the Elizabethan poor laws most relief to the poor had been in the form of payments of out-relief either in cash or kind but under an act of 1715 the provision of parish workhouses was encouraged in which many of the able-bodied poor could be placed and provided with work, albeit of a menial and repetitive nature, as an alternative to out-relief. Some parishes adapted existing buildings as workhouses, others entered into agreements with local tradesmen and industrialists to take on poor people in their workshops, but at Chesterfield a purpose-built workhouse was erected, paid for by public subscription. The major subscribers towards "the building, erecting or purchasing of a suitable and convenient workhouse within the Borough of Chesterfield for maintaining, employing and setting to work the Poor and Indigent people of the Borough" were almost entirely members of the ancient families of burgesses who dominated the corporation, the vestry and the manor court in the eighteenth century. John Bright was the leading subscriber with £100, but the Milnes, the Soresbys, the Slaters, the Heathcotes, the Inmans, the Allwoods, the Watkinsons, the Websters and so on, were very much in evidence in helping to amass the £494 collected in 1734[12]. Every person who subscribed over £10 was eligible to act as a trustee, so that the first list of trustees had a very familiar ring to it

As always, the building of the workhouse in South Place was an "inside job", the work being undertaken by Richard Milnes who was also a subscriber and a burgess. The quantities of materials involved were large and a substantial proportion of the population was concerned with the supply and carriage of bricks, stone, lime, timber, sand and slate, in what was a major piece of public works. Among the expenses was the cost of a journey to Mansfield to view the workhouse there, Joseph Shipston producing a drawing and plan for £2 2s 0d which suggests that the final form of the building owed much to its Mansfield counterpart.

There are no surviving overseers accounts for Chesterfield and the operation of the complex laws of settlement, bastardy and apprenticeship that were refined over the course of the eighteenth century, is represented only by a handful of stray documents in a private collection[13] and by reference to disputed cases in the

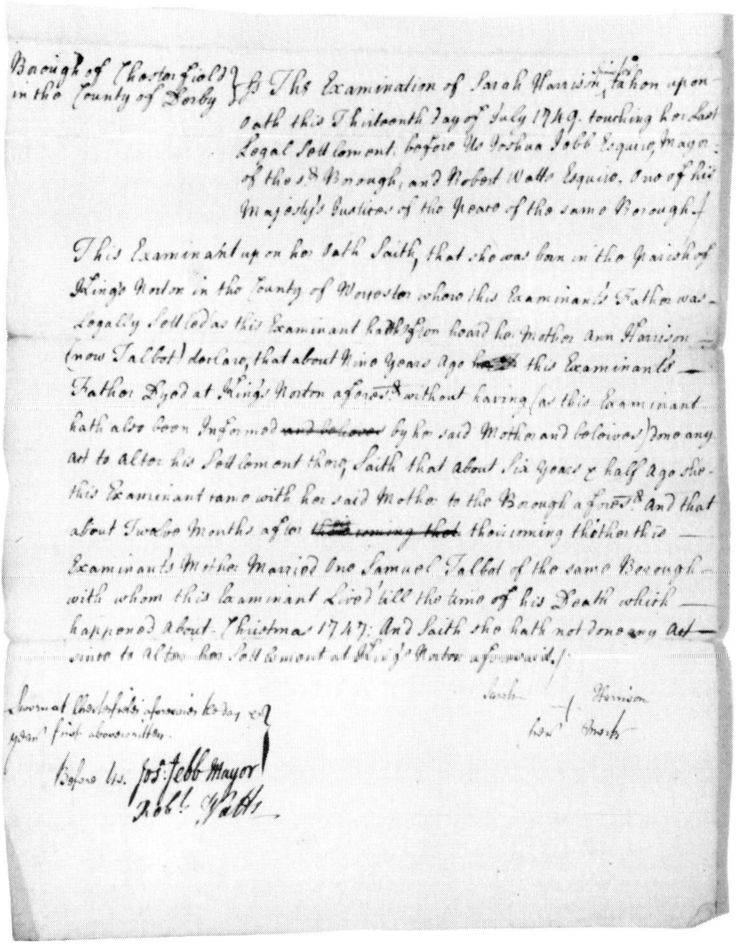

Borough of Chesterfield } ss
in the County of Derby }

The Examination of Sarah Harrison Spinster taken upon Oath this Thirteenth day of July 1749. touching her Last Legal Settlement, before Us Joshua Jebb Esquire, Mayor of the sd Borough, and Robert Watts Esquire, One of his Majesty's Justices of the Peace of the same Borough.

This Examinant upon her Oath Saith, that she was born in the Parish of Kings Norton in the County of Worcester where this Examinant's Father was Legally Settled as this Examinant hath often heard her Mother Ann Harrison (now Talbot) declare, that about Nine Years Ago ~~[illegible]~~ this Examinants Father Dyed at Kings Norton aforesd without having (as this Examinant hath also been Informed ~~and believes~~ by her said Mother and believes) done any Act to Alter his Settlement there; Saith that about Six Years & half Ago she this Examinant came with her said Mother to the Borough aforesd. And that about Twelve Months after ~~[illegible]~~ their coming thither this Examinant's Mother Married One Samuel Talbot of the same Borough with whom this Examinant Lived till the time of his Death which happened about Christmas 1747: And Saith she hath not done any Act since to Alter her Settlement at Kings Norton aforesaid.

Sarah Harrison
her mark

Sworn at Chesterfield aforesaid the day and year first abovewritten.

Before Us. Jos: Jebb Mayor
Robt. Watts

Settlement examination of Sarah Harrison, 13 July 1749

quarter sessions order books for the county. A register of settlement examinations was known to exist in the 1950s[14] but its present whereabouts is unknown.

Under the laws of settlement, a poor person moving into a town or village was unlikely to be allowed to remain there unless he was in possession of a certificate issued by his legal place of settlement acknowledging his settlement there and offering relief in the event of him falling on hard times. Such poor people were John Allen, his wife and four children, Richard, Dean, James and Ann, who moved from Calverton, Nottinghamshire, to Chesterfield in July 1784[15] presumably in search of work. The overseers of Calverton promised to receive the family back should they request relief elsewhere.

If people likely to ask for poor relief turned up in the town without such a certificate, they were likely to be hauled before two of the local magistrates and questioned as to their place of legal settlement. Where they survive in number, the settlement examinations, as the documents arising from this process are known, provide fascinating insights into the lives of the labouring poor in

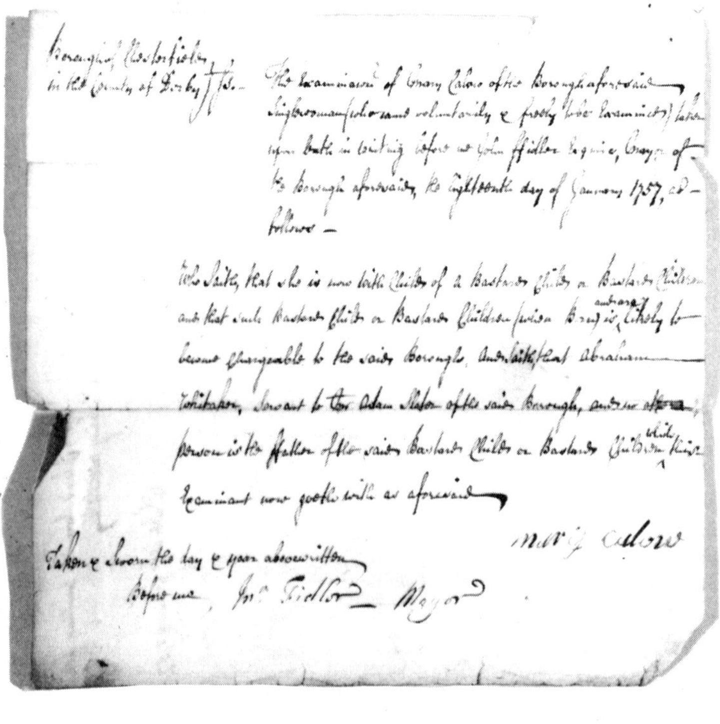
Borough of Chesterfield in the County of Derby } ss.
The examination of Mary Calow of the Borough aforesaid Singlewoman (who came voluntarily & freely to be examined) taken upon oath in writing before me John ffidler Esquire, Mayor of the Borough aforesaid, the eighteenth day of January 1757, as follows –

Who saith, that she is now with child of a Bastard child or Bastard children and that such Bastard child or Bastard children (when born) is likely to become chargeable to the said Borough. And saith that Abraham Whitaker, servant to Adam Slater of the said Borough, and no other person is the ffather of the said Bastard child or Bastard children which this Examinant now goeth with as aforesaid

Mary Calow

Taken & sworn the day & year abovewritten before me, Jno. ffidler Mayor

Bastardy examination of Mary Calow, 18 January 1757

the eighteenth century in particular. Apart from the missing 1817–1836 register, only three such documents have so far been located for Chesterfield[16] and not one of them is a particularly good example as they fail to provide the type of interesting potted life history that they can be expected to give. However, that of Edward Cowley, examined before Robert Marsden, the mayor, and an unnamed justice 8 May 1782 is of some interest. He was born at Stonegravels and lived there with his father until the age of ten when he went out to service and worked for a variety of people without gaining any further settlement. In 1771 he had enlisted in the 37th Regiment of Foot, being discharged in 1781 with no income other than being an "out-pensioner" of the Royal Hospital of Chelsea. As he had been born in the parish, Cowley would doubtless have been allowed to remain and receive relief.

A settlement examination and a removal order survive for Sarah Harrison, examined before Joshua Jebb, mayor, and Robert Watts, justice, 13 July 1749[17]. As she was born in Kings Norton, Worcestershire, it is not surprising to find that a month later she was removed there having failed to prove to Jebb and Watts that she had performed one of the five "acts of settlement" that would have allowed her to remain in the town.

The very considerable amount of documentation arising from the bastardy laws is represented only by three bastardy examinations[18], the first stage in a very lengthy process. The most interesting case of the three is that of Mary Hodgkinson, examined before the mayor, Samuel Towndrow, 13 January 1768: she gave birth to a girl in the workhouse, the baby dying when a week old. She named William Paylin, a cordwainer from the town, as the "putative father", and the examination states that the costs of lying-in, the midwife, maintenance of mother and child and the child's funeral had been borne by the inhabitants of Chesterfield. If the baby had survived, Paylin would have had to pay a weekly sum to the parish (not the mother) for the child's maintenance and education, and to enter into a bond to indemnify the parish against the costs and charges arising from bringing up the child.

Although the main archive for administration of the poor laws continues to be absent, three sources become available in the closing years of the century that throw a little more light on the life of the poor in the town and on the arrangements for their welfare at a time when the pressure on a system set up two hundred years previously for a much smaller, essentially rural population, was intense. The vestry minutes for the parish of Chesterfield are, as we have seen, available from 1782[19] but are singularly uninformative on the whole regarding poor law matters and in no way compensate for the loss of the main body of poor law papers. One suspects that among the lost papers are the records of a "select vestry" set up to deal with poor law matters alone in 1817, as from that date the already infrequent references to the day-to-day running of the poor laws become even less frequent.

Such references as there are relate principally to the appointment of officers. On 6 October 1784 Samuel Watts and his wife Elizabeth were appointed master and mistress of the workhouse at a combined salary of £10 per annum: this followed the resignation of Elizabeth Revel "the present mistress". Elizabeth Watts was appointed "keeper of the workhouse" on the death of her husband in 1797 and she also received his salary. She died in 1800 and was replaced as governor by John Cartledge. In 1816 the method of managing the workhouse took another turn when the post of manager was apparently combined with that of assistant overseer, John Draper being appointed assistant overseer and he and his wife managers of the workhouse at a combined salary of £50, with a deduction of £6 per annum for every child Mrs. Draper might have whilst remaining in the workhouse.

In 1826 there was another change in its administration when it was decided that the management of the workhouse should be carried on under the inspection of a governess at an annual salary not exceeding £20, and such governess "to act from time to time" under the immediate control and direction of the overseers and committee (presumably the select vestry). As a result of this decision, John Draper was required to resign as manager of the workhouse but retained his position as assistant overseer at an annual salary of £60 per annum. The level of this salary suggests that the paid assistant overseers did much of the day-to-day work of poor law administration. A decision of the vestry meeting taken in April 1797 had reflected the ever-increasing pressure on the overseers, it being agreed that "Samuel Thacker and Joseph Gratton ought not to serve any other parochial offices for the end of the ensuing year because of the extraordinary trouble they have had as overseers of the poor last year".

On 20 March 1826 we have one of the few insights into life at the workhouse provided by the vestry minutes when the overseers and the committee were empowered to make such alterations in the workhouse and premises that might be necessary in order to bring about the future separation of the male and female paupers therein as they shall think most conducive to their morality and comfort as well as benefit to the town, and that the expense be paid out of the poor rates". One is tempted to speculate whether such a major reform of internal arrangements within the workhouse had anything to do with the arrival on the scene in 1822 of the formidable Thomas Hill, vicar, and later archdeacon, of Chesterfield.

In 1831 there was another change in policy – what would now be described as a U-turn – when in August of that year the vestry discussed the propriety of altering the present government of the workhouse by having "an overseer and wife to act as matron and assistant overseer". This resolution was accepted and Thomas Gratton was appointed as an assistant overseer who would devote the whole of his time to the duties of the workhouse at a salary of £60 per annum: he was appointed 1 September 1831 and it was Gratton who took the workhouse into the era of the Chesterfield Poor Law Union.

These glimpses of workhouse life from the vestry minutes are greatly amplified by the account of the workhouse given in the entry for Chesterfield in Eden's *State of the Poor,* Vol.II, 1797. The workhouse was described as being in a good situation, being "clean and sufficiently spacious". There were eight or more beds in each room, each bed being filled with chaff, with two sheets, a blanket and a coverlid. The inmates when sick were removed to a small adjoining building, in which were also lodged lunatics and persons labouring under infectious disorders. This categorisation, together with the proposed division into sexes referred to above, sets it in a favourable light relative to some later union institutions. There was a large work-room where the inmates were largely employed in spinning lint and wool for household consumption, an activity that was said to realise a modest £30 a year. Able-bodied men were sometimes sent out to work.

There were 28 inmates of the workhouse as distinct from 41 people receiving out-relief in 1797, some two per-cent of the population therefore being in receipt of poor relief in some form. The workhouse population consisted principally of the very old and the very young (mainly illegitimate), with no men of working age at the time of the report. The weekly diet was predictably monotonous, bearing more than a passing resemblance to that in the later union workhouse. Breakfast was invariably milk pottage, whilst the dinner was a rotation of bread, beef, broth and potatoes, puddings, sauce and beer, and bread, cheese and beer. Supper was a rotation of broth and bread, beer and bread and bread and butter. One stone of beef was allowed to thirty persons and three ounces of cheese to each adult person. Wheaten bread, described as "very good", was provided. The sauce sounded less appetising being a mixture of water, vinegar and treacle.

Such was life in the workhouse. From time to time the vestry minutes provide tantalising snippets on other aspects of poor law affairs at this date. The only reference to an apprenticeship matter is at the meeting of 16 November 1785 and it was certainly a very unusual one: the meeting considered whether to put John son of Francis Machin apprentice to Samuel Goodlad of Sheffield to learn to play the violin: six of the meeting voted in favour, three against. In 1826 a considerable amount of time was devoted to a different matter, namely the question of producing a new map and valuation of the parish for poor rate purposes. John Gratton of

Wingerworth was elected to make the valuation and map although,confusingly, it was stated at an earlier meeting that George Glossop had successfully tendered. The valuations for Hasland, Tapton, Newbold and Calow survive[20], as do the maps for Hasland and Chesterfield[21]. In 1827 it became clear that a select vestry was indeed in operation as a committee of twelve was elected to “assist the overseers of the poor of that year”.

Eden had stated in 1797 that Chesterfield was extremely reluctant to grant settlement certificates and on the eve of the Poor Law Amendment Act in 1833, the subject of keeping to a minimum the number of poor gaining settlements was being discussed by the vestry. In that year it was resolved to remind the inhabitants that all servants must not be hired for longer than 51 weeks “so as to prevent settlements being gained by persons who ought to be settled elsewhere”.

Annual summary expenditure on the relief of the poor in Chesterfield is theoretically at least available from 1774[22] but Eden found it difficult to distinguish what part of the sum levied by the poor rate was actually spent on the poor as distinct from being diverted to the bellman (town crier), the beadle etc. However unreliable the actual figures, the general trend over the 1774–1795 period is nevertheless clear (see Table 4) with net expenditure rising to over £400 for the first time in 1780, over £500 in 1783, over £600 in 1786 and over £700 in 1789. Generally speaking, expenditure in the 1790s was roughly double that in the 1770s, indicating the increased pressure on resources in the closing twenty years of the eighteenth century.

From 1801 to 1817 much more detailed figures on the amount of poor rate collected and the uses to which it was put are available as a result of a return which quarter sessions was obliged to make to parliament in 1817, giving details of expenditure on the relief and maintenance of the poor in each poor law district[23] (see Table 4). Apart from revealing a continuing trend towards increased expenditure, with major watersheds in 1801 (above £1000 net expenditure for the first time), 1813 (above £2000 for the first time)and 1817 (above £3000 for the first time), this short run of statistics provides other points of interest. Not least of these is the erratic amount of poor rate levied from year to year, with a minimum of £1178 in 1807 and a maximum of £3421 in 1817. This was partly, but certainly not wholly, due to understandably erratic expenditure on the militia, with 1804, 1808, 1811 and 1813 standing out as the unstable years in the Napoleonic Wars period. Considering the stereotyped nature of many poor rate assessments, such wide variations from year to year are rather surprising: the trend towards increased poor law expenditure is by no means an even progression from year to year.

Table 4 Poor law expenditure in Chesterfield 1774–1817

	Poor rate	*County charges (gaol etc.)*	*Militia*	*Church rate*	*Salaries of overseers*	*Net expend-iture on poor*
	£ s d	£ s d	£ s d	£ s d	£ s d	£ s d
1774						334 12 7¾
1775						321 10 7
1776						333 9 6
1777						328 6 7
1778						347 4 6
1779						332 17 6
1780						409 9 3
1781						469 10 4½
1782						449 2 4½
1783						567 2 4½
1784						531 17 5½
1785						500 6 0
1786						653 5 4
1787						546 18 1
1788						676 5 8
1789						711 19 0
1790						575 15 9¾
1791						596 15 7½
1792						567 15 7
1793						588 1 0
1794						586 18 2½
1795						680 8 3½
1801	1615 1 3½		32 3 6		15 0 0	1053 8 9½
1802	1595 19 6¾	19 16 6	67 2 10	48 8 6½	21 0 0	1376 15 3¾
1803	1784 0 10½	35 9 6	157 14 11	21 4 5	21 0 0	918 4 5½
1804	2093 15 6½	45 17 7½.	872 4 7	48 13 10½	21 0 0	1059 17 0½
1805	1426 2 10	35 17 0	73 9 6	70 19 6	21 0 0	1195 8 10
1806	1247 11 10	23 6 3	38 15 4	50 13 3	21 0 0	1060 1 2
1807	1178 17 2	38 10 8	40 0 2	23 1 3	21 0 0	964 18 5
1808	1820 0 0½	39 14 7	429 1 6	22 4 6	18 0 0	1483 9 2½
1809	1788 14 1½	67 19 8	112 4 0	34 5 8	18 0 0	1452 5 1½
1810	1691 12 8½	32 1 0	77 17 5	29 18 0	22 0 0	1465 16 3½
1811	2032 11 10½	72 1 9	267 2 2	14 4 0	38 0 0	1802 14 10½
1812	1832 12 8½	8 9 0	63 10 3	35 0 3	38 0 0	1602 15 1½
1813	2977 0 1½	42 19 2	154 11 2	41 1 6	43 0 0	2539 3 9½
1814	2620 6 8½	91 2 11	21 4 4	27 9 5	88 0 0	2249 12 10½
1815	2849 17 2	78 19 6	18 18 4	28 3 10	88 0 0	2519 12 0
1816	2257 12 6½	61 14 4	74 6 8	32 18 4½	88 0 0	1930 18 10
1817	3421 8 9½	76 18 9		66 15 2	76 0 0	3035 2 4½

Notes on Table 4

1774–1795 is based on figures given in Eden's *State of the Poor*, Vol.II, 1797.

The figures for 1801–1817 are based on a return to parliament of poor law expenditure in Derbyshire Quarter Sessions records, Derbyshire Record Office, QAGr 242.

The totals for net expenditure 1801–1817 do not tally with the sum that is arrived at after the deductions from the poor rate total because legal expenses also have to be deducted.

The post-1813 increase in net expenditure is abundantly clear however, with the lowest 1813–7 figure (£1930 in 1816) well above any previous figure. It was in this period above all, with people serving in the armed forces returning from active service, the post war depression and a much increased urban population, that the strain on the poor laws became really acute. The 1817 enquiry on expenditure was, in fact, part of the process that eventually led to poor law reform in 1834. The overseers in 1817 were involved in expending nine times the amount of money their counterparts forty three years earlier had spent, and the ratepayers of the borough must have been acutely aware of the mounting pressures on the system.

The contribution of post Restoration charities

Charities continued to form an important supplement to poor relief in the seventeenth and eighteenth centuries as philanthropically-minded citizens continued to add to the long list of Chesterfield charities. Over the years the corporation became trustees of many of them and, as we have seen, the way it administered the charity monies and the charity property came in for a great deal of criticism culminating in the saddling of the reformed corporation with a debt of over £700 following investigation by the Charity Commissioners in the 1820s.

Some seventeen charities were set up between 1664 and 1802 many of them involving charitable distributions to the poor at stated times and two of them requiring the provision of almshouses. The earliest of the charities, that of Thomas Large set up by his will of 16 June 1664[24] was one of the more important, benefitting the church, the poor and the grammar school. An almshouse was built west of the churchyard on land purchased from Thomas Slater for £10 10s 0d on 26 December 1702. It was to be occupied by three widows or old women, chosen by the corporation, who were to have £5 per annum and every Christmas "one new gown of blue colour". In 1826 the building was reported to be kept in good repair by the corporation. Rents issuing from a variety of properties were also to provide for monthly distributions of bread to the "poorest people", for the repair of the parish church, for payments to the master of the grammar school and for a payment to the vicar for preaching two sermons.

The slightly later charity of George Taylor, founded by his will of 2 May 1668, had very similar provisions. Six one-roomed almshouses on Saltergate were provided for respectable poor widows chosen by the corporation, and they were granted small allowances of cash, bread, coal and blue gowns. His will likewise provided for the distribution of bread each Sunday to twelve poor housekeepers – £2 12s 0d per annum being set aside for this purpose – and, more originally, provided 8s per annum for the repair of the road from Durrant Hall to the parish church and Market Place.

Many other charities provided gifts of bread, money, shoes, stockings and gowns to poor people to the extent that by about 1700 the distribution of these charitable bequests must have been a complex operation in practical terms with almost a need for a "charitable calendar" to keep abreast of which distribution was due. Bread, for instance, was distributed monthly to the "poorest people" under the Large charity, to twelve poor housekeepers every Sunday under the Taylor charity, to three poor people every Sunday after morning service under the charity of Samuel Sleigh (1684), weekly to four poor widows in the market under the charity of Richard and George Youle (1699) and weekly to six poor widows under the charity of Nicholas Youle (1702). In other words there were several opportunities, even weekly, for nominated poor people to receive free bread. Both the Youle charities and the Moore charity (Francis Moore 1715) provided for gifts of shoes and stockings for the poor at Christmas.

The charity of Ann Heathcote and her sons of 1710 had the rather different aim of apprenticing poor boys whose parents did not receive relief from the poor rates. This was a type of charity that was set up quite often particularly in urban areas but was the only one in Chesterfield. This type of apprenticeship could often be confused in later years with genuine parish apprenticeships of poor children.

Cumulatively, the town's charities constituted a not insubstantial and now frequently forgotten additional income for various categories of poor, in particular the old and poor widows, and some at least had the advantage of not being subject to anything akin to the laws of settlement and therefore potentially available to some people who did not qualify for relief from the parish. The combination of charitable donations to the welfare of the poor is hard to quantify but the sheer number of charities in Chesterfield suggest that for some people at least these would have been a significant factor in maintaining a tolerable standard of living.

The other work of the vestry

As it was the Statute of Labourers that was initially responsible for the development of the parish as a civil authority, one would expect highways to figure prominently among the work of the vestry. Once again this is not so: apart from the appointment of the surveyors, little is recorded most of the time and, as in the case of the poor laws, large quantities of documents have been lost[25]. The first reference to a highway matter does not, in fact, occur in the vestry minutes until 1795 when on 23 January it was recorded that the Silk Mill Bridge was in a ruinous condition and it was resolved that three-quarters of the repair expenses should be paid by the inhabitants of Chesterfield and one quarter by the inhabitants of Hasland. The next notable highway event came in 1821 when it was decided to pave and lay causeways in the "new street called Soresby Street" where the first national school had been built in 1813.

In the closing years of the period the question of the repair of the turnpike roads crops up with increasing frequency as the trustees of hard-up turnpikes attempted to ensure that statute duty was carried out on the turnpikes or the appropriate composition money paid. In April 1832, for instance, the surveyor of the Chesterfield-Worksop turnpike road had issued a summons signed by two magistrates requiring that the Chesterfield surveyors deliver a list of the inhabitants of the town liable to do statute duty on the road. The vestry was not co-operative: the list was refused on the grounds that the section of Tapton Lane in the borough boundaries was "part of the town" not part of the turnpike. In December 1832, on similar lines, the parish surveyors were insisting that they must be allowed through the St. Helens gate and Ashgate bars free of charge when carrying materials for the repair of highways in the town. The statute duty system was by this time on its last legs, of course, for, as with the poor laws, reform was only a few years away, and it is interesting to see the turnpike authorities raising the issue when paid labour had become the norm.

The few surviving detailed accounts for road repairs for the Worksop turnpike road provide interesting asides on the costs of labour and materials in the 1820s[26]. The usual wage for men working on the road seems to have been 2s 6d per day – 10s per week – for those actually working on the repair of the road. Those doing less-skilled work received less – for breaking stones Joseph Richardson received 8d per load in 1827. Characteristically, no great sophistication in the mode of repairs is suggested by the accounts: it was really just a question of "getting" loads of stone locally (Handley Quarry is mentioned), breaking it and filling in the holes. The accounts suggest that to provide some sort of consolation for carrying out one's statute duty, in Chesterfield at least, there was ample "statute ale". £2 13s 0d of the £20 0s 6d expended on the repairs to the Chesterfield-Worksop road in September 1827 was a payment to John Shipman for "statute ale".

The vestry was also responsible for the appointment of a number of town officials – the town crier, the beadle and the apothecary – and references to these appointments and the conduct of these officers crop up from time to time in the minutes. In 1802 Samuel Tetley was sacked as town crier for his misdemeanours. In June 1805 it was reported that Mr. Brown, the town's apothecary, had been overpaid £25 and it was ordered that in future the limit for the annual bill of medicines should be £25. In 1820 Samuel Kirk retired as beadle after fifty years service and Thomas Grant, labourer, was appointed to replace him at £5 per annum and a pair of shoes, a new coat every two years and a gown where necessary.

Because of the continuing role of the manor court in the appointment of constables, there is little reference to the maintenance of law and order until 1831 when John Bower was appointed "General Constable" at a salary of £10 per annum. At the same meeting a pinder was appointed at a salary of £5 per annum and a lock-up house keeper for the same salary. In a few years time, the maintenance of law and order was to become the responsibility of the reformed borough council. During the Napoleonic Wars period much attention was paid to raising men for the armed services and to the raising of substitutes for the militia. As an inducement to joining the navy in February and March 1795, each volunteer was being offered a new round hat, a pair of trousers, a blue jacket and flannel waistcoat.

The most important business being dealt with in the closing years of the vestry as a major force in the government of the town was, of course, the provision of gas lighting for the town of which a full account is given in Volume III of the *History of Chesterfield* along with an account of the improvements in water supplies and other public utilities introduced in the 1820s and 1830s. The most important point to be made here is the fact that such a major step forward for the town should have been dealt with by the vestry and not by the borough although many of the same personnel were involved. The first meeting on the subject on 20 February 1823 was chaired by John Mugliston, many times mayor, and was also attended by other long-standing burgesses such as Samuel Dutton and George Batteson. The purpose of the meeting was to determine what number of lamps would be necessary to light the streets and public places and to settle what sum of money should be annually paid by the inhabitants for the same in order "that necessary provision in respect thereof may be made in the Act of Parliament". The meeting decided that eighty lamps were necessary and that the annual price should be £2 10s 0d per lamp per annum and that a rate called the "gas rate" should be annually laid by the surveyors of the highways upon all the occupiers of houses in the town, except those with an annual value of less than £4 10s

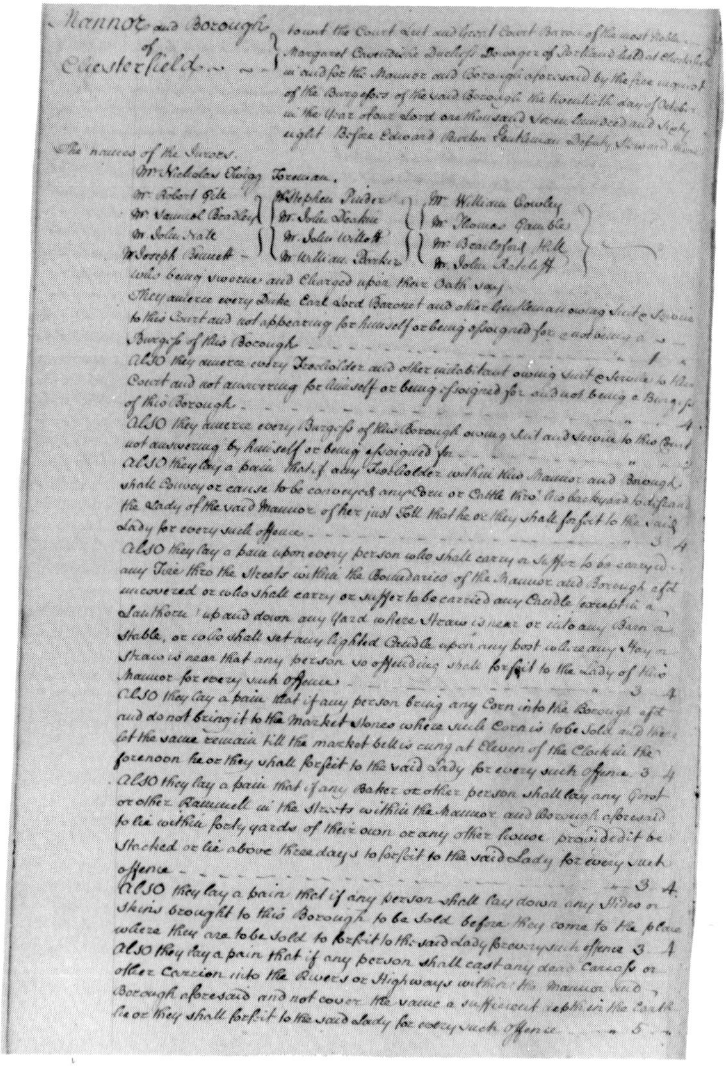

Mannor and Borough of Chesterfield — } The Court Leet and Great Court Baron of the most Noble Margaret Cavendishe Duchess Dowager of Portland held at Chesterfield in and for the Mannor and Borough aforesaid by the free request of the Burgesses of the said Borough the twentieth day of October in the Year of our Lord one thousand Seven hundred and Sixty eight Before Edward Burton Gentleman Deputy Steward

The names of the Jurors.

Mr Nicholas Clarig Foreman,

Mr Robert Gile	Mr Stephen Pinder	Mr William Cowley
Mr Samuel Bradley	Mr John Deakin	Mr Thomas Gamble
Mr John Nall	Mr John Wilcott	Mr Beresford Hill
Mr Joseph Bennett	Mr William Barker	Mr John Ashcliff

who being sworne and Charged upon their Oath say

They amerce every Duke Earl Lord Baronet and other Gentleman owing Suit & Service to this Court and not appearing for himself or being essoigned for and being a Burgess of this Borough — — 1

ALSO they amerce every Freeholder and other inhabitant owing Suit & Service to this Court and not answering for himself or being essoigned for and not being a Burgess of this Borough — — 4

ALSO they amerce every Burgess of this Borough owing Suit and Service to this Court not answering by himself or being essoigned for — — 2

ALSO they lay a pain that if any Freeholder within this Mannor and Borough shall Convey or cause to be conveyed any Corn or Cattle thro' his backyard to defraud the Lady of the said Mannor of her just Toll that he or they shall forfeit to the said Lady for every such offence — — 3 4

ALSO they lay a pain upon every person who shall carry or suffer to be carryed any Fire thro the Streets within the Boundaries of the Mannor and Borough afsd uncovered or who shall carry or suffer to be carried any Candle except in a Lanthorn up and down any Yard where Straw is near or into any Barn or Stable, or who shall set any lighted Candle upon any post where any Hay or Straw is near that any person so offending shall forfeit to the Lady of this Mannor for every such offence — — 3 4

ALSO they lay a pain that if any person bring any Corn into the Borough afsd and do not bring it to the Market Stones where such Corn is to be Sold and there let the same remain till the market bell is rung at Eleven of the Clock in the forenoon he or they shall forfeit to the said Lady for every such offence 3 4

ALSO they lay a pain that if any Baker or other person shall lay any Gorse or other Rammell in the Streets within the Mannor and Borough aforesaid to lie within forty yards of their own or any other house provided it be Stacked or lie above three days to forfeit to the said Lady for every such offence — — 3 4

ALSO they lay a pain that if any person shall lay down any Hides or Skins brought to this Borough to be Sold before they come to the place where they are to be Sold to forfeit to the said Lady for every such offence 3 4

ALSO they lay a pain that if any person shall cast any dead Carcass or other Carrion into the Rivers or Highways within the Mannor and Borough aforesaid and not cover the same a sufficient depth in the Earth he or they shall forfeit to the said Lady for every such offence — — 5

Opening proceedings of Chesterfield Manor Court, 20 October 1768

0d. This would raise an adequate annual sum to defray the expenses of eighty lamps or any larger number. It was resolved that the gas company should receive no more than 10 per cent upon their shares and therefore all profits made by the company above that annual percentage should remain in the hands of the treasurer of the gas company to be expended on alterations and improvements. The bill for lighting the town with gas was adopted by the vestry at the meeting of 10 February 1825.

The eighteenth century manor court

By the time we catch up with the manor court when the sole surviving court book for this period begins in 1763[27] the enforcement of the manorial bye-laws relating to the suppression of nuisances had become its chief business as the manor remained the principal authority in these matters. Even vestiges of feudalism such as the fining of people for non-attendance also remained however, although whether the court was able to enforce the payment of the fines it placed on all and sundry is another matter. Other important rights nevertheless remained, the most surprising in view of the town's status as an incorporated borough since 1598 being the control and supervision of the markets which remained in the hands of the lords of the manor until 1840, along with the rights of levying tolls on the corn and cattle sold there. The transcript of the proceedings of the court held 25 October 1787 (Appendix B) demonstrates all of these functions.

The court ceremonial in the eighteenth and nineteenth centuries also remained much as it always had been. In 1763 it was still styled the "Court Leet and Great Court Baron of the Most Noble Margaret Cavendish, Duchess Dowager of Portland, held at Chesterfield for the Manor and Borough aforesaid by the free Inquest of the Burgesses of the said Borough". By this time the court met only in October, and the jury of twelve consisted frequently of members of the corporation, with a foreman who had commonly been mayor in the preceding year. After 1787 it met in the new Town Hall which stood on the site of the present Midland Bank.

The amount of business dealt with by the court depended to some extent on the degree of enthusiasm of the officials. Between 1799 and 1817 when Robert Waller, the town clerk, was deputy steward, the recorded business declined to the mere appointment of manorial officals, but after 1817 when John Charge, a local solicitor, later to become clerk of the peace for Derbyshire, took over, the court underwent a revival. Several officials continued to be appointed, among them the constables. Generally, there were at least two, and in times of trouble any number of assistant

Table 5

Descent of the manor of Chesterfield 1660–1830

1660 William, Earl (from 1665, Duke) of Newcastle

|

1676 Henry, 2nd Duke of Newcastle

|

1694 John, 3rd Duke of Newcastle

|

1711 Edward Harley, 2nd Earl of Oxford
(m. Henrietta Cavendish d. of 3rd Duke of Newcastle)

|

1755 Margaret, Countess of Oxford
(d. and heir of 2nd Earl of Oxford, m. in
1734 William, 2nd Duke of Portland)

|

1771 William, 3rd Duke of Portland

|

1792 5th Duke of Devonshire (following exchange of
estates between the Dukes of Portland and Devonshire)

|

1811–1830 6th Duke of Devonshire

constables might be appointed, thirty-three in 1816 with the discontent at the close of the Napoleonic wars. Until 1776 when, according to Pegge, the old market house and market cross between the Market Place and New Square were pulled down, two "market lookers" continued to be appointed. The market buildings (the Markethouse, the Cage, the Market Cross and the Rails at the bottom of Glumangate) had in fact been reported to the court as "out of repair and dangerous" in 1764. A pinder was also appointed yearly to be responsible for the pinfold "at the bottom of West Bars".

The bulk of the business, however, involved the suppression of nuisances and the removal of common annoyances or dangers to the inhabitants of the town. The most frequent nuisances, especially in the earlier years, were the ashes, rubbish, refuse and dunghills which were spread in some profusion through the town streets, a situation that had not apparently radically altered since Tudor times. Local worthies such as the vicar continued to be offenders from time to time and in 1818 Back Lane was said to be impassable for rubbish of various kinds. Slaughterhouses and butchers shops were also frequent causes of complaints: in 1775 John Harvey was presented for sweeping "blood and guts" into the market place. The failure to scour ditches and watercourses was another characteristic offence of the time, as it was not until the 1830s that covered soughs and sewers began to replace open ditches for the disposal of waste and drainage.

Apart from these offences to public health, the court was also concerned with several dangers to life and limb from unsafe property. Cases of insecure tiles, slates, plaster, chimneys and dangerous projections such as shutters and inn-signs all occur in the court book and in 1836 a bye-law was adopted imposing a fine of 40s on all persons not having proper spouts and conductors for the removal of water from roofs. Overhanging trees were another problem, Anthony Lax Maynard of West House and Robert Malkin of Tapton Lane being presented for offences in this connection. Although roads and footpaths were the responsibility of the surveyors of the highways appointed by the vestry, the manor court from time to time reported cases of inadequate maintenance and requested the surveyors to take action. In 1822, a stretch of West Bars was said to be out of repair and dangerous and there were several complaints about the state of bridges – Wheatbridge (1768), Lordsmill Bridge (1770) and Silk Mill Bridge (1829).

All in all, the entries in the court book do not project a very attractive picture of central Chesterfield in the late eighteenth and early nineteenth centuries. The overall impression is of a great deal of neglected and dilapidated property and unhealthy and insanitary conditions, with ashes, refuse, dunghills, open sewers and ditches ever-present features of the overcrowded town centre.

CHAPTER 3

THE CREATION OF WEALTH

At whatever date between the mid seventeenth and early nineteenth century one examines the pattern of trade and industry in Chesterfield, its most obvious feature is the contrast between the area of the ancient borough which continued to be dominated by the craft and workshop industries, epitomised by the leather trades, which were so characteristic of medieval boroughs and market centres, and the periphery where even in the mid seventeenth century mineral-based industry was already well-developed. The nearest the coal industry came to the borough was the coal-pits on Newbold Road and at Boythorpe[1], whilst the Smiths' eighteenth century ironworks brought the iron industry to within a matter of yards of the borough boundary.

The "Scarsdale economic survey" of the Commonwealth period[12] demonstrates succinctly the extent to which coal, iron, and, to a lesser extent, lead had already taken hold of the neighbouring villages with a coal delph and two lead mills in Brampton, two furnaces, a hammer and slitting mill in Staveley and Barlow, a coal delph and furnace in Wingerworth, a coal delph and four lead mills in Walton, five coal delphs in Dronfield and one coal delph at Calow. Chesterfield was already at the centre of a flourishing industrial area without participating directly in this industry itself. Its importance as the market centre for north east Derbyshire remained undiminished throughout, the very wide range of retail and service industries reflecting this position. As an alleged market centre for the lead industry, its position is less clear with direct involvement limited to a small number of wealthy merchants.

It was characteristic of the type of industry that dominated the borough that among the principal developments of the seventeenth century should be the establishment of five trading companies to regulate many of the traditional trades of the town[3]. The earliest was the Company of Shoemakers, followed in 1626 by the Company of Tailors and Sadlers and in 1629 by the Company of Butchers. The Company of Smiths and Braziers followed in 1648 and finally in 1677 the Company of Mercers was established to include drapers, grocers, apothecaries, dyers, hatters, clothworkers, hosiers and weavers, as well as mercers. Because of the lack of records of the companies, apart from their ordinances, their influence on the economic life of the town cannot satisfactorily be assessed.

Some of the ordinances of the Company of Butchers dating from 1629 are known and they serve to demonstrate the constitutional position of such a company within the borough as well as to illustrate the regulation of their particular trade. Such ordinances of a trade or craft association had to be approved by the crown in order to safeguard the public interest, and those for the Company of Butchers were allowed by the Justice of Assize for the county of Derby on 29 June 1629. The preamble recites that the Master, Wardens, Fellowship and Company of Butchers within the borough of Chesterfield petitioned the mayor and corporation for these ordinances. How long the company had been in existence before this petition was considered by the corporation at the Guildhall on 6 March 1629 is not clear, but presumably not for very long as the first major task of a company after its formal constitution would be to frame a code of rules for the regulation of its trade. The corporation, after a conference with most of the butchers, agreed on the need "for the better ordering and governance of the trade", formally issued these ordinances. No butcher was to kill any pork for sale in the Shambles between May Day and Martinmas Day on pain of a fine of ten shillings. The sale of diseased, rotten or unwholesome flesh in the Shambles was punishable by fines of ten shillings for beef, five for pork and two for mutton. Butchers and victuallers, not resident in the borough, were allowed to sell their meat or victuals in the town between 8 a.m. and 4 p.m. or in the summer 5 p.m. A fine of two shillings threatened any butcher who dressed "any mutton after the manner of lamb, whereby the buyer thereof may be deceived". When a butcher was recognised as a master of the trade, he was to pay a fee of 6s 8d to the mayor, such payments to be devoted to the purchase of corporation plate. The master of the company was empowered to distribute money from a fund raised by its members for the relief of "poor decayed men of the same trade". These are the only known ordinances of this company; they provide no details of its constitution, apprenticeship arrangements or restrictions on the practice of the trade.

Records of the Company of Tailors and Sadlers are similarly fragmentary. They consist of a number of ordinances approved by the corporation including those in response to a petition, dated 9 November 1649, from the tailors and sadlers for the confirmation of "certain old customs and ordinances", presumably those shown in illustration number 8. In these trades an apprentice had to be

Part of the orders made by the Borough of Chesterfield for the conduct of the affairs of the Company of Tailors and Sadlers, 20 December 1626

legally bound to his master for at least seven years but an indenture prepared by the town clerk and enrolled before the mayor. Nobody who was not a burgess or had not served an apprenticeship in the borough could practice these trades without paying a composition fee to the mayor and to the company. The interests of the tailors and sadlers resident in the borough and consequently liable to the payment of its rates were further protected by an order forbidding the employment of any "country tailor" which would prejudice their work, "provided that tailors inhabiting the borough be sufficient and able workmen". A burgess offending against this order would be fined 13s 4d and any other inhabitant 10s. A tailor was required to work at the house of any inhabitant who gave him six days notice, except during the fortnights before Christmas, Easter and Whitsuntide when they were free to finish work undertaken in their own houses. Failure to comply with this order would make the tailor liable to a fine of 13s 4d payable to the corporation unles remitted by the customer. No tailor or sadler was to work on Sundays nor was he to allow his servants or apprentices to do so on pain of a 10s fine. All journeymen in this trade were to pay quarterly dues of fourpence to the company for the relief of the poor, sick, lame and impotent

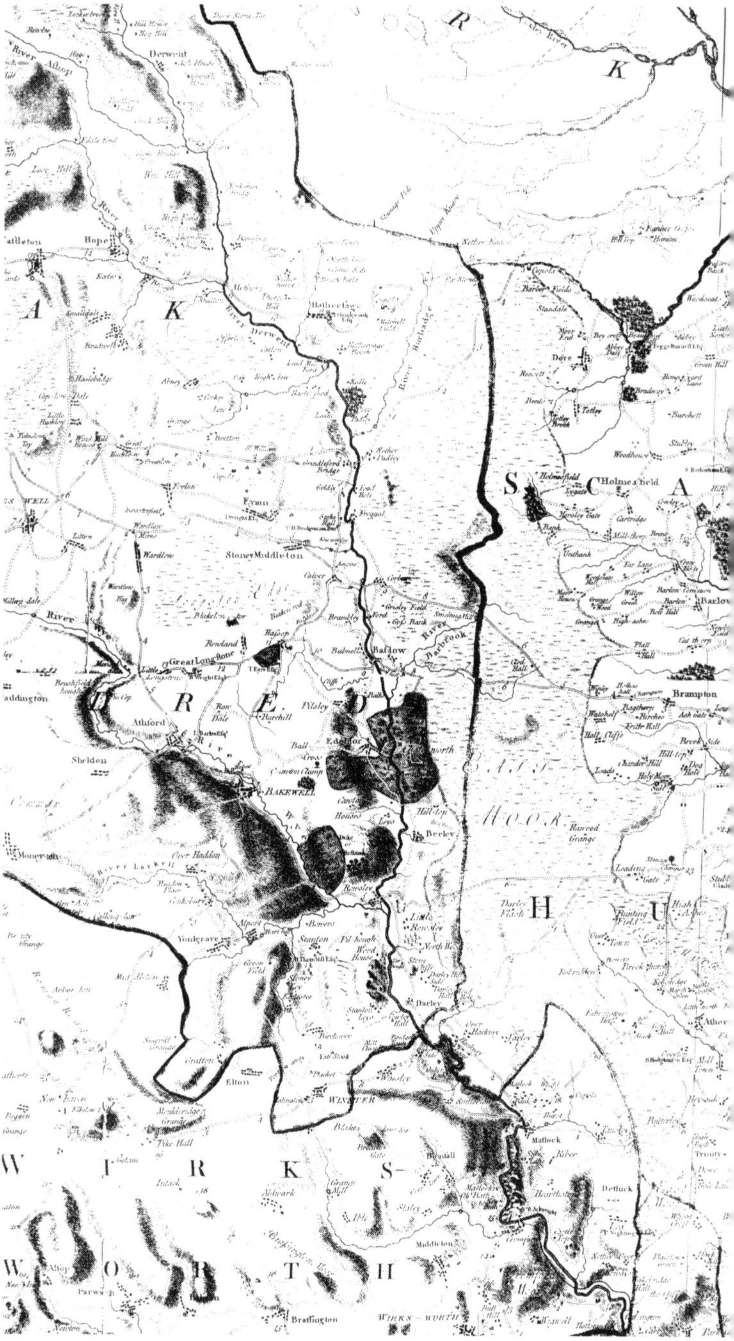

Fig.2 Chesterfield in its setting 1791

Engraved by Thos. Kitchin Hydrographer to his MAJESTY
Chesterfield Canal to the River Trent
River Rother
Beighton
Wales
Harthill
South Anston
Eckington
Barlborough
Stavely
Woodthorp
Clown
Elmton
Whitwell
WORKSOP
BOLSOVER
Scarcliff
Upper Langwith
Shirebrook
Pleasley
Newbold Mill
MANSFIELD
Skegby
Sutton
Tibshelf
Blackwel
ALFRETON
South Normanton
Kirkby
Pinxton
Norwood
Whaley
Cuckney
Church Warsop
Market Warsop
Clipstone Park
North Wingfield
Normanton
Heath
Palterton
Glapwell
Hardstoff
Brimington
Killamarsh

in these occupations; any failing to do this would be disqualified from employment by members of the company.

More information is available for the Company of Mercers. It was formally established by the corporation on 24 July 1677 and was governed by a steward, two wardens and ten brothers. These officers were then nominated: Richard Marchant, mercer, as steward; Edward Wood, apothecary, and Hugh Wheldon, grocer, as wardens; and as the brethren, Edward Ward, mercer, Francis Moore, grocer, William Dowker, draper, Thomas Ludlam, mercer, William Inman, grocer, Thomas Radford, mercer, Samuel Bright, apothecary, James Ludlam, grocer, John Smith, hatter, and Robert Story, dyer. The steward could appoint a registrar to record the company's bye-laws and decrees, and a beadle to summon meetings of the company. The steward, wardens and brethren were to elect a new steward and wardens each year, to fill any vacancies among the brethren by co-option from among "the discreetest, honestest and ablest persons" in the trades represented in the company. They were authorised to make orders for the regulation of these trades, provided that they were not in conflict with the laws of England or the privileges of the lord of the manor, Henry, Duke of Newcastle. Apprenticeship lasted seven years from the date of its entry into the company's register. The two wardens could enter any shops or warehouses of people in the company's trades before 10.00 a.m., except on market or fair days, to inspect weights and measures and to check that their goods, wares and merchandise were "good, merchantible and vendable". Every member of the company had to attend the annual election wearing his gown or cloak; on that day the steward, wardens and brethren were to pay a shilling each and the other members fourpence into the company's funds. The business of the company was to be kept secret. Members were to behave respectfully to the mayor and aldermen of the borough as well as to their own officers. Before anyone apprenticed to a member could become a freeman of the company, open a shop or practice his trade, he had to be approved by the officers of the company and presented to the corporation to be sworn in as a burgess; breaches of this rule were to be punished by a fine of £5 a month payable to the company. The weaving of jersey stuffs and their sale, except on market days, were strictly limited to burgesses, the fine against this order being sixpence for every yard woven or sold. Members of the company were restricted to the trade or handicraft to which they had been apprenticed, although in certain circumstances a change might be made with a licence in writing from the mayor and aldermen. Finally, no tailor in the borough could offer for sale any trimming, wares or commodities for the making up of a garment, except for the finishing of clothes made for his own customers.

It is apparent from these orders of the trading companies that one of their main objects was to prevent strangers, both masters and workmen, from following trades in Chesterfield. This protectionist policy was fully backed up by the corporation. An order made in November 1648, for example, imposed a special levy on strangers coming to live in the town and on landlords who accommodated them[4] until they could give sufficient security to the corporation or left the town. In the following August these payments were fixed at ten shillings for a landlord and five shillings for a stranger, and to enforce this order the town was divided into six wards, each under an alderman who had to inspect his ward and prevent strangers from living there and non-members of the trading companies or guilds from trading. A memorandum of February 1657 defined these wards, unfortunately in many cases by reference to houses which cannot now be located precisely. Mr. Clay was responsible for an area "from Mr. Hill's house down the Nether Rowe within the Westbarrs to Widdow Elizabeth Fletcher's"; Mr. Wood for "the Upper Rowe to John Smith's and Mr. Gervase's house and then down by the Bull to James Lambert's; Mr. Needham for the Market Place and Church Lane; Mr. Forth for Glumangate, Knifesmithgate and the Narrow Lane; Mr. Wayne for a long stretch from "the Potthouse beneath the Chappel Schole" along Holywell Street and down "Marygate to Mr. John Wheldon's"; and finally Mr. Reginald for Lordsmill Street (not mentioned by name) as far as the bridge, Beetwell Street and Vicar Lane to his own house.

These trading activities were taking place in a town where it was still the market itself that caught the outsider's eye. A survey of Derbyshire made in the reign of Charles II has the following comment[5]:

> "Here are weekly two Markets, the one on Tuesdays, formerly held in the old Market-place, but long since neglected; and the other on Saturdays, which is kept in the large new Market-place, being very considerable for Corn, Lead and all Country Commodities."

Despite this mention of lead, Blome gave Wirksworth the accolade of being "the greatest Lead-market in England"; he also mentioned lead in relation to Bakewell's Monday market.

Contemporary local references to the market and fairs are those made by Leonard Wheatcroft of Ashover in his diary[6]. For instance, on 28 July 1670 he wrote: "I went to a faire at Chesterfeild where I staied all night"; on 28 February 1671, "that day being Chesterfeild faire day, I, like a bad lad, went to it and staid there all night"; a year later he recorded his purchases, "There I did buy of one Richard Kemp 52 quarters of malt, and a horse of John Buxton my brother; the malt was at 20s the quarter all that yeare; t'horse price was 37s"; and in 1682, "I went to

Chesterfeild faire, where I lighted upon another dame one Mary Jenings" to whom he bound his daughter Elizabeth apprentice for two years. Other visits were for equally diverse purposes: on 18 June 1670 "I went to Chesterfeild to louse (redeem) some goods I had pauned 2 years before and brought them home"; on 17 July 1697, "I and my doughter went to Chesterfeild to buy some household goods, when Richard Stringfellow broke"; and a little later, "My next journey was to Chesterfeild, July 8, with the Church Bible to get it bound". Leonard Wheatcroft was then seventy, a man who had been a tailor, soldier, parish clerk, alehouse keeper, gardener, carpenter, poet and school teacher, and who lived for another ten years before he died and was buried as he had directed in a stone coffin at Ashover.

Some years after Wheatcroft's time, there was one of the periodic wrangles between the inhabitants and the bailiffs of the lord of the manor regarding the market. In 1770 the bailiff, John Cooper, moved the corn market from its customary position and set up stalls in its place[7]. A number of inhabitants, led by Robert Thornley, Richard Allwood, Richard Wilkinson and Stephen Gamble petitioned the Duke of Portland for a return to the old arrangement. Their petition is tersely endorsed "to be removed back, if refused to give notice to quit". This matter was presumably settled to their satisfaction but in January 1771 another petition signed by 58 townsmen was sent to the Duke complaining of Cooper's abuse of his position as lessee of the manorial tolls of Chesterfield. Their request for an enquiry was granted and from the resulting award something can be learnt of the details of the market tolls at this time. The toll for wheat, beans, peas, rye and other grain, except barley, was to be a Winchester quart for three strikes and for oats a Winchester quart for four strikes. The reason for the lower rate on oats is not certain nor is it clear why no toll was to be taken for barley, except for seed. Vehicles had been charged at a penny a wheel, though the justification for this levy was doubtful as the Duke did not repair any roads. Cooper had been the first to take tolls on turnips, grass and clover seed, but this demand required further investigation. Cheese would be "a great object" in the trade of Chesterfield when the canal was open, and this it was submitted made it particularly important that the toll on cheese should be twopence or threepence a cartload as at Mansfield, Derby and Nottingham, and not the 6s 8d a ton that Cooper had taken nor the customary toll of 3s 4d a ton.

The importance that contemporaries attached to the market function of the town was also seen in the opposition by the trading community to improvements in transport elsewhere which might have resulted in a diversion of trade from routes through Chesterfield. Such a scheme was that for the improvement of the navigation of the Don from Sheffield to Doncaster[8] and then by the

Dutch River to the Ouse at Goole. This project, initiated in the 1690s, suffered various setbacks before 1726 when a bill sponsored by the Company of Cutlers from Sheffield was steered through the House of Lords by the Duke of Devonshire. In 1732, the Sheffield and Doncaster interests were combined in an act which established a new Don Company. Some of the stoutest opposition to the navigation came from Bawtry because of the threat to its position as an important inland port serving the industries of south Yorkshire and north Derbyshire, in particular the transport of lead from the Peak District to the Humber. Chesterfield was, of course, located on this route and some at least of its traders were as opposed to the project as those in Bawtry. In 1722 Thomas Lister, lord of the manor of Bawtry and one of the most determined opponents of the Don navigation, wrote to Joseph Mellish who was busy organising opposition in Parliament:

> "I cannot find out how Lord James Cavendish is affected, tho I am told that Chesterfield are jealous of losing their market to Sheffield and therefore not very fond of the navigation. Mr. Bright who was mayor of Chesterfield last year, signed a petition then against it. Great many of Lord James's tenants are lead carriers this way, and must suffer on that account".

Later that year he reported:

> "Chesterfield has refus'd to come into the project and are very jealous of Sheffield. . .".

In February 1723 he made another reference to the attitudes of Chesterfield people:

> "Mr. Dempster was also at Chesterfield, where they are uneasy at it and have promised him to sign a petition against it. Tomorrow I shall send them a form and desire the lead merchants to send with the petition a letter to their members to desire them to espouse it, which I hope may have some effect on Sir James Curzon and Lord James, for Mr. Bright, Mr. Mills [Milnes] and the principall merchants there will sign the petition".

The trade was not all one-way, however, as is made clear by other correspondence. In 1722, for instance, Thomas Lister wrote to Joseph Mellish:

> "Mansfield and Worksop and other towns send great quantities of malt into Derbyshire, which trade will be entirely lost and all commerce between Nottinghamshire and Derbyshire, which is now commodious by the cheapness of sending goods back in the carts which bring lead this way, will be at an end."

The opposition obviously came from strongly entrenched interests and the potential benefits of the Don navigation to the Derbyshire economy at this time could not be seen. The exploitation of the county's mineral resources had always been handicapped by the difficulty of transporting these heavy goods to navigable water in the Trent Valley. The 4500 tons of lead said to be produced within seven miles of Sheffield and the large numbers of millstones were perhaps the outstanding examples, but there was marble and rotten stone, and coal, to be added. There could also be a considerable saving on road maintenance as the main roads were "torn in pieces by lead, iron, millstones, marble and other heavy carriage".[10]

In the seventeenth and eighteenth centuries Chesterfield's role in the communications pattern of the north Midlands as a market town where a major east to west traffic route crossed one of the main routes from Yorkshire and the north to the Midlands and the South was indeed as important as ever. There are many examples in this period of the reluctance of parishes in the Chesterfield area to continually foot the bill for this heavy mineral traffic much of it of non-local origin and it was appropriate that the first road in the Chesterfield area to be improved by a turnpike trust should be part of the main east-west route from Bakewell to Chesterfield and Worksop which traditionally carried the lead traffic to Bawtry. The act of Parliament setting up the trust was passed in 1739. The other major routes into the town – the Matlock road (1760) and the Derby road (1759) – also belonged to the first generation of Derbyshire turnpike trusts.

For all these changes and would-be changes, when we arrive at the structure of industry in the town in the better-documented mid eighteenth century, we find the picture little changed from the era of the foundation of the trading companies. The church rate assessment of 1744[11] provides a detailed picture of industry in the town in this period. Numerically, tanyards and malthouses were the predominant manifestation of traditional Chesterfield industry with an alarming concentration of five tanneries on Lordsmill Street on the lower reaches of the Hipper and the Rother. Not all the streets are named in this assessment but in general principle the greater concentration of industry appears to have been in the southern part of the town – Low Pavement, Packers Row, Beetwell Street, Lordsmill Street – with some of the streets in the northern half of the town, notably Saltergate and Glumangate almost purely residential. Retail premises and small workshops abounded, of course, throughout the central area. Overall, nine tanneries are listed and eight malthouses. Four of the tanneries appear to have been in the Low Pavement area and one can only hope that they were at the river end of the long plots stretching down from the market place. Combine these tanneries with the great concentration of butchers shops in the Shambles and one can begin to see why the eighteenth century town must, in part at least, have been less than a pleasant place. What is not clear from the 1744 assessment is the extent to which the hosiery industry, which was important in the town by the end of the century, had

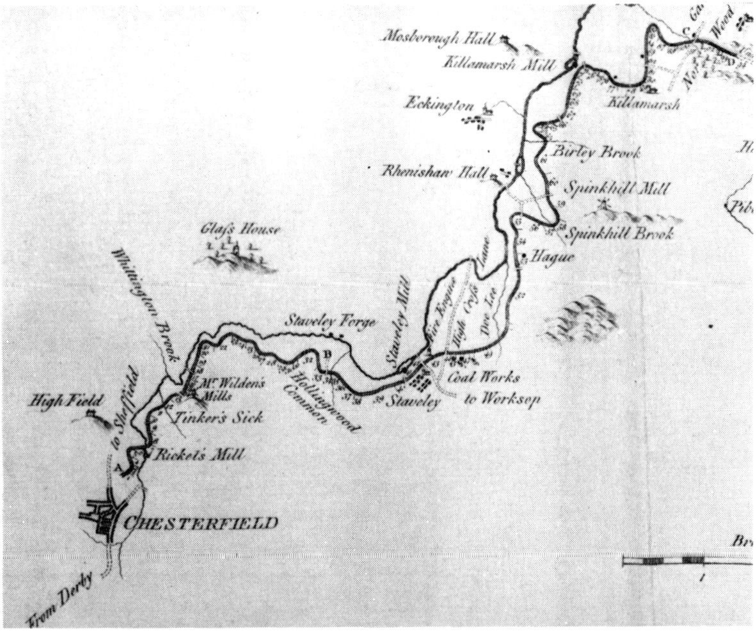

Part of the plan of the proposed Chesterfield Canal, 1769

developed by this time. As a domestic or small workshop industry, stocking-shops would not be differentiated. The names involved in eighteenth century industry have a familiar Chesterfield ring to them – the Allwoods, Milnes, Wingfields, Websters, Brocksops in the tanning industry; the Friths and Woods in the dyeing industry; the Wingfields, Barkers, Thackers and Woods in the malting industry.

The whole range of sources that come together towards the end of the century confirm the basic picture provided in 1744. The opening of the Chesterfield Canal in 1777 had little direct impact on the industrial structure of the town, the only innovations totally attributable to the canal being the appearance of two canal carriers, Daniel Hill and Co. and John Storrs and Co.[12] The canal was in general terms more of a boon to the mineral-based industries of the hinterland, than to the labour-intensive workshop industries of the town centre.

The other noticeable change over the course of the eighteenth century was the growth of the hosiery industry. Four manufacturers of hose are recited in Bailey (Jebb and Bower, Charles Kinder, Richard Natt and John White) and Pilkington, writing in 1789[13] refers to the manufacture of stockings as one of the main industries of the town. The 1783 Directory confirms, however, that numer-

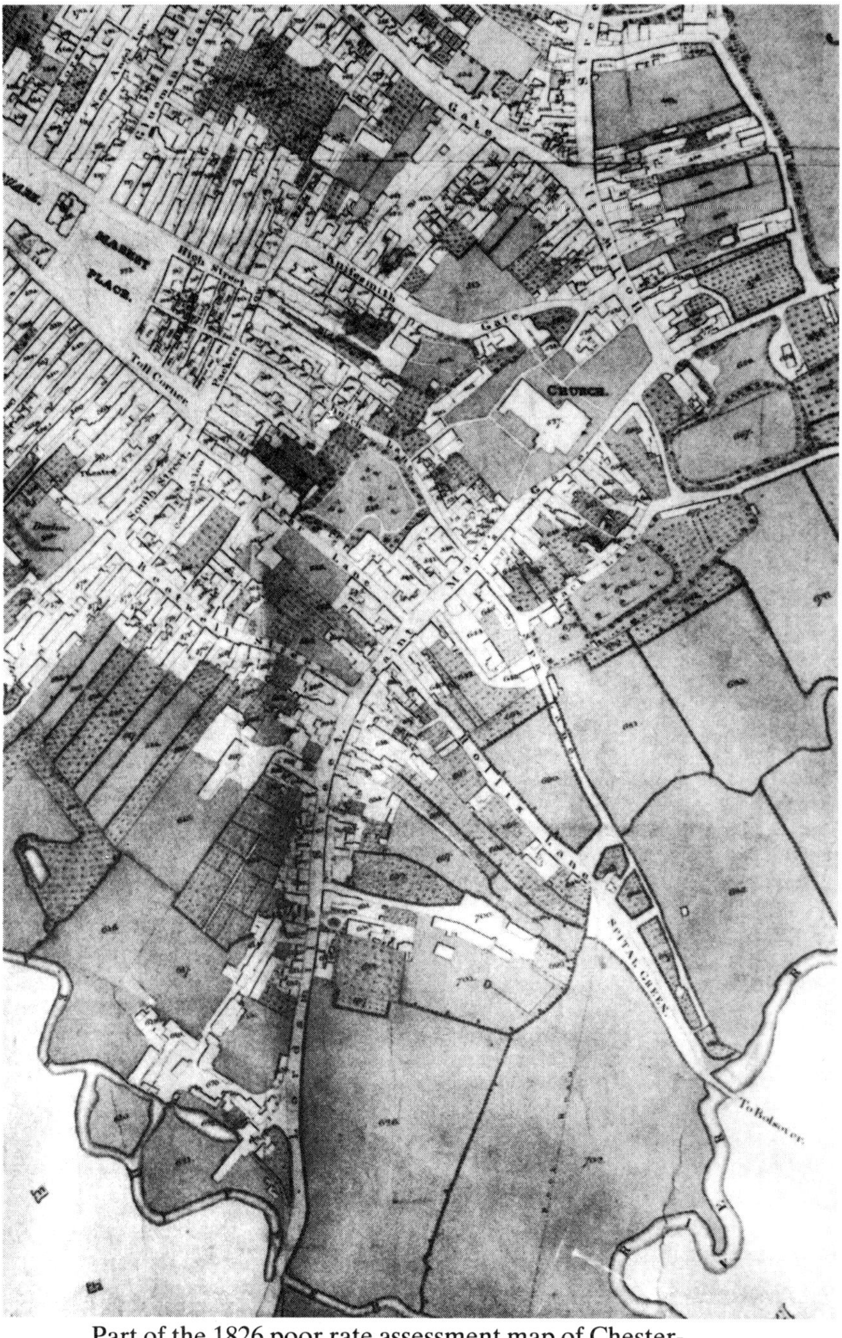

Part of the 1826 poor rate assessment map of Chesterfield showing the area around the silk mill

ically tanning was still holding its own with five tanners listed (Joseph Bower, Samuel Bower, Joseph Routh, John Smith and Godfrey Webster) and Pilkington refers to the importance of the manufacture of shoes in the town for the London trade. Two lead merchants, Bernard Lucas and Joseph Storrs, are listed in the Directory, and Stephen Gamble, a ropemaker: according to a later church rate assessment[14] the rope walk was situated on Knifesmithgate. There continued to be large numbers of malthouses and candlehouses dotted throughout the town, and two ancient pillars of the Chesterfield industrial scene, the two corn mills – the Lords Mill (leased from the Duke of Devonshire by Mr. Slack in the early 1800s) and the Bishops Mill (belonging to the Dean of Lincoln) on Bishops Mill Lane, continued to function.[15]

It is not until 1786 that Chesterfield's first factory, William Tucker's silk mill on Beetwell Street appears in the land tax assessments[16] (assessed at the not insubstantial and easily recognisable sum of £1 5s 11¾d) although it has traditionally been attributed to an earlier date by virtue of a datestone of 1759 said to have been incorporated in the building. By 1820[17] the property consisted of the mill itself, Tucker's house and 28 tenements for workers at the mill.

Pigot's *Commercial Directory of Derbyshire* of 1835[18] confirms the pattern of industry in the early nineteenth century town. Numerically boot and shoe makers (39) were well and truly dominant, followed by the always ubiquitous butchers (23). The tanners were now reduced to three, concentrated on Lordsmill Street, while there is no reference to hosiery manufacture which presumably died out over the opening decades of the century. There were still eleven maltsters, but the tallow chandlers were down to three in number. The range of retail trades and workshop industries remained as wide as ever with most trades and crafts represented as you would expect in an important market town: there were 20 tailors, 17 grocers and tea dealers, 14 dressmakers, 11 stone masons, 10 joiners, 8 braziers and tinplate workers and 8 blacksmiths, and overall the picture is of a thriving commercial community based on the type of craft, workshop and retail trades that had long dominated the town.

If trade and industry in central Chesterfield proceeded in its almost timeless way, this was hardly true of the periphery where the burgeoning coal, iron and pottery industries developed rapidly from the late eighteenth century onwards boosted by the technological advances of the Industrial Revolution. The most important development of this period took place just over the western boundary of the borough in Brampton where in 1775 John Smith, a member of a prominent Sheffield family of cutlers, in association with two Sheffield ironmongers Samuel Allsop and John Ernest Sanor, acquired a furnace, foundry, boring mill and forge and thus laid the foundations for the Brampton or Griffin Ironworks.[19] The furnace and foundry were taken on a 999 years lease from James Shemwell. The lease also mentions a bellows house with rooms above, a counting house, smithies, a grinding mill and other buildings "lately erected", together with a "fire engine"[steam engine] built on a plot of ground adjoining the corn mill known as Walton Nether Mill, worked by James Shemwell. The building known today as Cannon Mill on Furnace Lane formed part of the original furnace premises. The boring mill and forge were leased at the same time from Samuel Johnson, Edward Wright and William Robinson, the owners of a tobacco pipe works in Wheatbridge Road. The second lease included the recently-made forge dam on the south side of Wheatbridge Road, whereas that made with James Shemwell carried with it only the right to take water from his corn mill dam. An interesting point to emerge from these first leases is the extent to which the complex of industrial buildings and watercourses between Wheatbridge Road and Boythorpe Road, near the junction of the Hipper and Holme Brook, was developed prior to 1775.

The new partnership did not have a smooth start because of "many and sundry difficulties occasioned by living at such great distance". By provisional agreement of 1776 therefore, William Robinson and John Cooper, an innkeeper, were brought in as partners in the hope that their local knowledge would help to make the concern profitable, but Robinson withdrew before the end of the year and Cooper shortly after. In a later agreement in 1776 the partners in addition to John Smith and Samuel Allsop are named as Thomas Biggin, a scythesmith of Norton, Richard Clarke, a Norwich ironmonger, and Thomas Munton of West Wretham, Norfolk, described as gentleman and ironmonger. This link with Norfolk is somewhat unexpected and the question arises as to whether it resulted from the growing demand in that county for agricultural tools and machinery combined with the improved link to the east coast via the new Chesterfield Canal. Munton moved to Chesterfield and Samuel Allsop was replaced by John Bale, a Chesterfield ironmonger, whilst in 1777, John Smith himself went to live at Wheatbridge House which he took on a long lease from William Robinson its builder. By 1782 Richard Clarke had also moved to Brampton. This concentration of the partners in the neighbourhood of the works was designed to secure more effective direction of the business in its formative years.

John Smith died in 1784 at the age of fifty-six. He was a man of strong religious beliefs and soon after moving to Brampton he was appointed a trustee of the newly built Independent or Congregational Chapel, known as the Blue Meeting House, in Froggatt's Yard below New Square. John Smith's eldest son, John, was relatively inconspicuous in the business. He lived at Field House,

Brampton, which he bought in 1801 from Benjamin Thompson, a moulder.

It was, in fact, John Smith's third son, Ebenezer, who was the most important figure in the history of the Griffin foundry from the 1780s until his death in 1827. He was educated for the nonconformist ministry and had formed his own Independent congregation in London at a meeting house in Fetter Lane when he renounced this calling in order to take part in the management of the family business. He moved to Brampton shortly before his father's death when he established his own increasing family, ultimately numbering eighteen, in Wheatbridge House.

The Griffin works had continued to develop after the early stimulus to iron production given by the American War of Independence. It was well placed to exploit the even greater demands for iron to be made during the prolonged wars from 1793 against France, with immediately local supplies of coal and iron. The Smiths owned coal mines in Staveley and the nearer Boythorpe Colliery. Ironstone was available in Ashgate, Brampton, Walton, Wingerworth and Hady. In the 1806 list of Derbyshire iron furnaces[20] the Griffin works with a production of 1700 tons a year was preceded only by Butterley with 1766 tons.

From the earliest years it is clear that cannons and cannon balls were major products of the firm. During the Napoleonic Wars 1200 workers were employed by Ebenezer Smith at what must have been the peak of the firm's activity and this aspect of its work is perpetuated in the name Cannon Mill. The demands for munitions in the 1790s encouraged the opening of the Adelphi ironworks at Duckmanton, ajdacent to plentiful supplies of ironstone.

Dependence on the needs of war, however, carried economic risks and it is interesting to see how, after the cease of hostilities, attempts were made to extend the range of the firm's products. In the late 1780s Ebenezer Smith, in association with Francis Thompson of Ashover, an accomplished engineer, developed the production of steam engines and pumping machinery. They regularly did work for Boulton and Watt of Birmingham and an outstanding example of their work, the pumping engine which operated for 125 years at Pentrich Colliery, is to be seen in the Science Museum at South Kensington. Another innovative product were the cast iron beams which were supplied in large numbers to the Strutts for supporting the floors of their new West Mill at Belper which was completed in 1795[21]. In the same decade Ebenezer Smith himself erected a three-storey building at the Griffin foundry incorporating cast-iron columns and beams: the building is now used as offices.

The firm's most widespread and continuing influence however, seems to have been through the great number of its products which helped to improve the standards of everyday life. Most prominent perhaps were the ordinary domestic cooking ranges and the more ornamental iron grates which found a place in innumerable houses from the humblest to the grandest. Cast-iron pans, frying pans and kettles were also produced in large numbers, and the constant aim to find new or extended uses for iron was reflected in the production of doors, stairs, balustrades, railings, stable racks and mangers, garden rollers, pipes, launders and stoves, such as the massive one purchased by the vestry in 1820 for £50 to heat the parish church.

With this wide range of products marketing assumed increasing importance. A journey book for the years 1824–35[22] shows how the partners in turn travelled to different parts of the country both to seek orders and to collect payments for goods supplied. In 1824, for instance, Joseph Bright Smith, travelled by express stage coach to London where he spent some time before making a tour of the south and west with calls at Brighton, Bristol, Birmingham and many smaller towns. The journey lasted 61 days and cost £53 17s 0d, whilst the money collected amounted to £3905. In view of the early connection with Norfolk it is interesting to see that one circuit was in East Anglia with visits to 45 towns as far south as Stowmarket and Bury St. Edmunds in 60 days. Other regular journeys were made into the Birmingham area, Yorkshire, the north east and, once a year, Ireland. After 1824 it was a case of diminishing returns from the journeys, receipts falling from £15564 in 1824 to £7228 in 1829.

Ebenezer Smith died at the age of seventy in 1827 and the works were soon to run into rapid decline although this could hardly have been apparent at the time. Indeed, when Sir Richard Phillips visited the works in 1829[23] some 3600 tons of iron were being produced annually – about one sixth of Derbyshire's production– and some 500–600 people were employed at Brampton, Adelphi and Calow together. He recorded that " the wages of the mechanics vary according to circumstances from 16s to 40s; and of the labourers from 10s to 15s per week". Yet within four years the Brampton ironworks had reached its end and the property was being sold.

CHAPTER 4

IN SCHOOL

The story of the development of educational provision in the town in this period is dominated by the Tudor grammar school. The history of the grammar school has been researched several times[1] and little can be added to the well-known but incomplete outlines of its development up to 1843 when it was revived by the reformed borough council. The school archives for this period are almost totally non-existent.

Little is known about the conduct of the school in the seventeenth century. The first recorded headmaster is Gilbert Allsop c.1618. Other seventeenth century headmasters are just a succession of names – Mr Gibson (mentioned 1624 and 1631), Mr Bonner (1633), Mr Wilby (1641,1643), Mr Stone (1653,1663 and possibly up to 1668), William Foxlowe (1691)[2] – with nothing known about them. The method of appointing the headmaster is illustrated by a petition dated 28 May 1634[3] from the mayor and corporation to the archbishop of York. It recites the clauses in Godfrey Foljambe's will by which he bequeathed 20 marks (£13 6s 8d) for the payment of a schoolmaster appointed by the archbishop, records that this sum had since been increased by other benefactions to £20 and submits the name of Thomas Bonner, B.A., schoolmaster of Rotherham, as a suitable person to fill the existing vacancy. He was to carry the petition to York where he was presumably interviewed by the archbishop. One question that arises from Godfrey Foljambe's bequest is why episcopal or rather archiepiscopal approval should be sought from York rather than from Lichfield or Canterbury. The explanation may be found in the source of the income allotted to a schoolmaster; it was derived from the estates of the rectory of Attenborough in Nottinghamshire and so within the diocese and province of York.

According to Pegge the school buildings were closed between 1691 and 1699[4] and the classes were held at the house of the Rev. William Sleigh, the schoolmaster, who was also rector of Shirland. In 1709 the school building was so dilapidated that it was dismantled and replaced by a brick building of two storeys, one the school and the other the master's residence[5]. The Rev. Robert Browne had succeeded Sleigh as headmaster in 1699 and among his pupils was Thomas Secker, later archbishop of Canterbury[6]. Browne was in turn succeeded by the Rev. William Burrows and the Rev. Saunders who was for a time co-headmaster. It was during Burrows' long term of office between the 1720s and c.1752 that the school was reputed to have become one of the leading educational establishments in the north. In 1733 no less than nine boys went from the school to Cambridge[7] among them Dr Samuel Pegge, the Rev. Ellis Farneworth, translator of the works of Machiavelli, Dr John Jebb, an eminent eighteenth century physician, and the Rev. Ralph Heathcote, a prebendary of Southwell.

There were two further charitable bequests in favour of the school in this period. In 1738 John Bright bequeathed the income of three closes in Ashover to the teacher of a petty school – to teach ten girls and ten boys of poor people in the town. In 1742 Leonard Gill left £1 7s 0d per annum (the interest on a capital sum of £30) to the free school in Chesterfield.

After the heyday of the eighteenth century school under the Rev. Burrows, it apparently entered an era of slow decline out of which it did not emerge for the remainder of this period. The Rev. Saunders co-headmaster with Burrows died in 1773 and the Rev. Joseph Shipstone, headmaster from 1773 to 1794, was a sick man all his life, so that the school languished for much of this period. On 1 September 1794[8] the Rev. Thomas Field, usher since 1781, was elected to replace Mr Shipstone and Mr Jowitt was elected schoolmaster of the petty school, a position in which he was to continue "so long as he shall behave himself in the same". The number of scholars at the grammar school at this time was as low as eight or nine and Mr Field also held the position of curate of both Barlow and Brampton. It is not surprising therefore that at the Charity Commissioners' enquiry towards the end of his "reign" he was accused of spending less than two hours a day at the school. Until 1803 Field was drawing the salary of usher as well as master. An order of the borough council of 24 June 1803[9] laid down that the salary should be placed in the hands of Mr Wilkinson and put at interest until a proper usher was appointed. Field suffered another blow in the same year when his salary was suspended because of the money expended by the corporation on the school house. In September 1803[10] Thomas Dutton, junior, was elected schoolmaster of the petty school. Field's salary for 1802 was eventually paid, but he failed in 1804 to persuade the corporation to restore the usher's salary to him[11].

The next flurry of activity began in 1822 when in March of that year[12] the allowance made to the petty schoolmaster was increased to £30 from £25, made up of £17 5s 0d from the body of the corporation (burgesses and brethren) and £12 15s 0d from the mayor and aldermen. The basic purpose of the petty school was to supply the grammar school with the children who could read and write – the basic condition of entry. It is not at all clear where it was held, except that it was not in the grammar school.

In March 1823[13] the town clerk received a letter from Mr. Charles Ellison, clerk to the Commissioners for Charities, and thus began the long investigation into the affairs of the grammar school. It was ordered that the town clerk and chamberlain be authorised to attend the Commissioners and to produce such deeds and papers as "shall be thought proper for the purpose". In May of the same year the School Committee of the corporation was ordered to look over the school buildings to see what repairs were necessary to the school and the windows and roof of the school house: the neglect of these was another charge laid against Field. When the committee reported back in June, it was decided that the school windows should be leaded and repaired[14]. In September 1823 the death of Thomas Dutton, master of the petty school was reported to the corporation but it was decided not to replace him[15]. The post was suspended for the time being and the poor children continued with his widow Elizabeth at their home. She would be paid weekly for such tuition out of corporation funds. It is interesting to note that in the contemporary return for Chesterfield for Archdeacon Butler's visitation in 1823 only two children were reported to be attending the grammar school[16].

In 1829[17] notice was received from the Commission inquiring into charities announcing their intention of instituting proceedings against the corporation for the misuse of sums properly belonging to the grammar and petty schools. With misappropriation of the funds by the corporation and neglect of school affairs by Field, the position was so unsatisfactory by Field's death in 1832 that the school closed in that year and was not to reopen until 1843.

The study of the grammar school in this period is totally frustrating. While we know quite a lot about the personalities involved, particularly after 1790, we are left wondering how it was run, what number of pupils were involved in its more successful periods, and how much it contributed to the life of the town. Such evidence as there is suggests that even in its more flourishing periods only small numbers of children were taught there and certainly the basic curriculum of greek and latin would have been of little practical application in an industrial area at the turn of the nineteenth century.

What were the alternatives therefore? Did any of the vast majority of children in the town have any chance of any formal education? For most there would be no alternative: the children of the wealthy would go away to boarding school or be taught by a governess but the majority would be left to pick up what scraps of information they could from parents and elder brothers and sisters. Public elementary education did not effectively arrive in the town until 1812 with the foundation in that year of the Soresby Street National School. The story of the setting up of the National School is told in Volume III of the *History of Chesterfield*[18].

What did flourish in the town were a considerable number of private academies, some twenty according to a return to the House of Lords in 1833[19], although once again, it is difficult to do anything more than demonstrate their existence and even this is difficult before the advent of detailed county directories in the 1820s. In Glover's *Directory* of 1829 six such academies are listed: the Misses Boden, M.A. and J. Fidler, Narrow Lane (for girls), Ann Wall, Holywell Street (girls boarding), the Rev. Robert Wallace, Elder Yard (boys boarding), John Woodhead, Holywell Street, and Richard Woodhead, Holywell Street. By 1835 many of these had gone, demonstrating the short-lived nature of most of these establishments. Only the Fidlers' school in Narrow Lane seems to have had a long life. In general, only the occasional exercise book among someone's private papers survives as evidence of these institutions, their ephemeral nature making it difficult to detect them in official sources such as tax and rating records in the eighteenth century. Bernard Lucas was probably being educated at an early eighteenth century Chesterfield academy when he was using the "schooling book" (dated 1718) that has survived among the Pashley papers[20]. Like so many such exercise books of the day, it is concerned with calculations aimed at a commercial and business training, something of a contrast to the exclusively classical education provided by the grammar school. Lucas was, of course, a member of the well-known local business and landed family and could have been receiving tuition at home.

CHAPTER 5

RELIGIOUS LIFE

The Established Church

In 1662, John Billingsley, the Presbyterian vicar of Chesterfield was ejected for failing to read the book of common prayer: in 1817 two surveyors reported to the vestry that the crooked spire was dangerous and recommended that it should be pulled down. As far as one can judge from the snippets of information available, church life was hardly characterised by such dramatic events over this period but the lack of any continuous source prior to the churchwardens accounts for 1762 leaves much to the imagination.

The restoration of the Church of England was largely achieved by the 1662 Act of Uniformity. Amongst other things this act required all clergy to declare their assent to the prayer book as revised in that year, to renounce any idea of resistance to the king or his representatives and obligations imposed by the Solemn League and Covenant, and to undertake to confirm to the liturgy of the Church of England. Those failing to accept these conditions by 24 August (St Bartholomew's Day) 1662 were to be deprived of their livings and, if they continued to preach, to be liable to three months imprisonment.

One of the twenty-nine ministers ejected under this act was indeed John Billingsley, vicar of Chesterfield since 1653. He was born at Chatham in 1625 and ordained as a Presbyterian minister at St Andrew Undershaft church, London, 26 September 1649[1]. He had been presented at the Quarter Sessions in Derby in July 1661 for failing to read the book of common prayer. He had come to Chesterfield from Cumberland as a minister with clear Presbyterian views. Soon after his arrival he engaged in a disputation with the Quaker, James Naylor, an account of which is recorded in a pamphlet entitled *A defence of the scriptures* by Immanuel Bourne, the former rector of Ashover, whose daughter he had married two years earlier. After the death of Oliver Cromwell, like many Presbyterians he became very discontented with the republican regime and "prayed publickly for the king, when it was hazardous to do it", with the result that he was summoned before the Council in London to answer charges of misdemeanour. The same independence of thought was shown up to the time of his eviction, as a letter from the bishop of Lichfield to the bishop of London, dated 29 September 1662, shows:

> "At Chesterfield, the minister Billingsley I convented before me in Consistory. I convicted him by sufficient witness that in a farewell sermon August 23, he said that the prelatical Ministers, at least some, were put out for murder, drunkenness, whordom etc. – but such as himself for being too holy and too carefull of Religion".

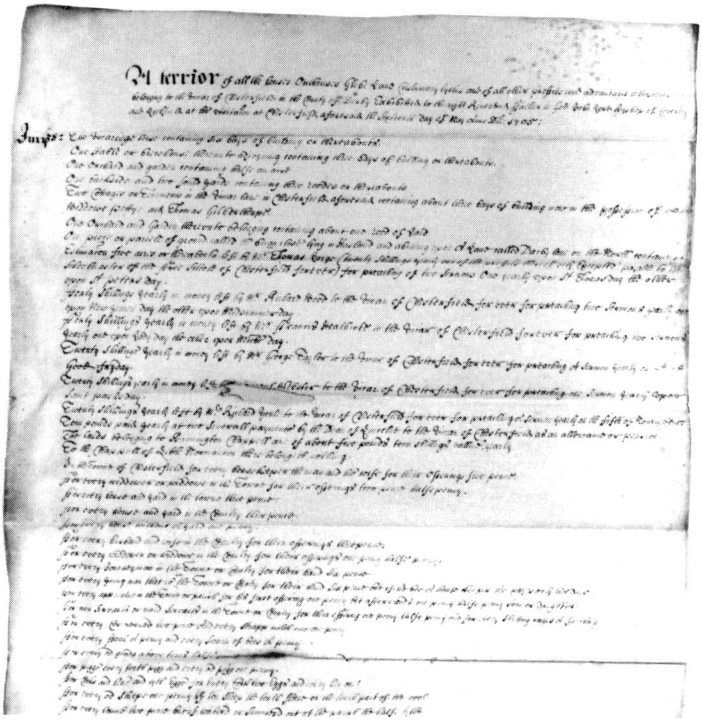
A terrier

Part of Chesterfield glebe terrier, 16 May 1705

His final sermon in the parish church must have been a spirited defence of his position, which he contrasted so forcefully with that of the Anglican clergy who had been deprived of their livings under the Commonwealth. He continued to live in Chesterfield working privately with some of his former parishioners until the passing of the Five Mile Act in 1665 made it impossible for him to do so.

Billingsley and his successsors depended for their livelihood on what seems to us a most curious set of tithes and customary dues[2].

Apart from the vicarage on Vicar Lane with its croft and orchard, the glebe was very limited consisting only of two cottages and a close of 6 acres, given by Thomas Large to the vicar of Chesterfield, called the Bridge Close, but 20s annually had to be paid out of its profits to the Grammar School. The vicarial tithes included customary payments for milch cattle (2d for every cow renned, 1d for every stropp milch cow), swarms of bees (1d per swarm), pigs (1d for every tenth pig and every odd pig), cocks and hens (two eggs per cock, one per hen) and geese($\frac{1}{2}$d each for every gosling above ten in number and every tenth goose). Unusually wool and lamb were included among the vicarial tithes, the vicar receiving a penny "for every odd sheep", and the fleece of every tenth sheep of a tenth part of the wool. The Easter offerings consisted of a scale of 1d to 6d, with every housekeeper paying 5d, a journeyman not a housekeeper paying 6d, but widows and widowers paid only 1$\frac{1}{2}$d and an apprentice only 1d for his first offering. There were also fees for burials and christenings and less obvious customary dues such as the 3s 4d payable by Brampton parish to Chesterfield for the privilege of burying the first person to die in Brampton in the new year at Brampton rather than Chesterfield, a recognition of the fact that Brampton was originally part of the parish of Chesterfield. The great or rectorial tithes were, of course, in the hands of the Dean of Lincoln who was rector of Chesterfield.

John Lobley, vicar of Chesterfield, died in 1694, one year after the making of the glebe terrier referred to above. His personal possessions are valued in his inventory[3] at as large a sum as £614, but of this total £500 is represented by debts owing to him, so the vicarage is rather less lavishly furnished and less extensive than such a total might at first suggest. The inventory in fact indicates a house of modest size with a hall, great parlour and kitchen on the ground floor and three chambers above them, also a cellar and a brewhouse. The hall contained a range with a few fire irons, eight chairs, two tables and a form, three carpets (table and other coverings), four cushions, a glass case and a pair of harpsichords. The great parlour also had a range with fire irons, as many as eighteen chairs, two tables, a featherbed, one carpet and two globes with their cases. The kitchen had rather more fire irons with its range and its "iron boyler", as well as an array of varied pots, pans, dishes, plates and drinking vessels in pewter, brass and iron. A warming pan, candlesticks, a looking glass and "two hollow smoothing irons and heeters" also had their place in a kitchen which had as its furniture a chest of drawers, a glass case, six chairs, a buffet stool, a dresser and shelves and an end board, but no table.

Upstairs, the white chamber had two featherbeds, a chest of drawers and three chairs, whilst there was another bed in the garret above. The chamber over the kitchen had a range, three beds, a table and six chairs, a press, a close stool and two boxes. In the green chamber were various pieces of furniture and furnishings that had been given to Mrs Hall, together valued at £1000. Linen valued at £7 15s 0d was listed separately, whilst the vicar's apparel and the money in his purse were worth £20. "Corn growing upon the ground" worth £8 was the sole evidence of any agricultural interests.

John Lobley had been vicar of Sheffield prior to coming to Chesterfield in 1681[4]. He was succeeded by two more Yorkshire-men, William Blakeman(1694–8), born at Rawmarsh[5] and Henry Audsley born at Worsborough[6].

As far as religious observance at this time is concerned, we know that in one respect at least it was more properly maintained in Chesterfield parish church than in many others in the eighteenth century: this was in the frequency with which holy communion was celebrated. It is known from a register of monies collected at communion services, analysed by Cox in 1890[7] but now unfortunately lost. The book dated from 1733 when Bernard Lucas and John Webster were churchwardens. At this time there were eighteen sacrament days in the year, that is the first Sunday in each month and Christmas Day, Good Friday, Easter Day, Low Sunday, Whitsun Day and Trinity Sunday. This pattern seems to have been very firmly established and to have persisted throughout the century under four different vicars. Within this pattern, a feature that according to Cox was unusual was the Good Friday celebration. "Chesterfield", he notes, "is one of the only instances that we have found wherein a continuous and largely attended Good Friday celebration can be proved right through the eighteenth century".

This register demonstrated that from 1733 the average amount collected on these sacramental occasions was about £14 for some years, but by the close of the century it had increased to £30. There was also a record of payments to the vicar, the curate, the clerk and the sexton. It seems probable that Chesterfield was one of the parishes where it had been customary to make an extra payment of 2s to these officers after every celebration of communion. How far this explains the frequency of communion in the curch can only be surmised, but at least the officers were given a financial incentive.

The money collected from these offerings constituted a separate fund from which the churchwardens were able to make allowances ranging from 6d to 4s to perhaps twenty people. At first the only details given were the names of the recipients but later some brief notes appeared, for example, in 1745 when 2s 6d was given to "Soldier Dowes motherless children" or in 1751 when.."a soldiers wife in the Glumangate" received 6d. From this time allowances were sometimes made in kind, 4s 6d for "a pare of shoose" in 1745.

From 1752 coal was bought and distributed to the poor, in 1755 a total of 167 loads costing £4 17s 5d. This form of poor relief was separate from and additional to both parish poor relief and parish charities. In various ways the churchwardens at different times added to these extra resources: in 1792 an "especial sacrament for the mayor and corporation" was arranged but their offerings yielded only a modest 6s 6d: three years later they "received of Mrs Smith for pigs being in the churchyard, 2s 3d". In this last decade of the eighteenth century the churchwardens seem to have obtained a steady income from fines imposed on erring parishioners. On 1 December 1793 five men each paid 10s fine for "suffering tipling in his house during divine service"; one was fined 5s for being drunk and others 3s 4d each "for tipling". When in that same year William Parker had to pay 5s to the churchwardens "for being in liquor", he generously gave an extra shilling as "his own addition for Almshouses in the Saltergate". In 1796 Joseph Glossop paid a fine of 5s for "leading cows on the Sabath day" and in 1803 they actually secured a shilling as a fine for swearing. After these references to the income derived from fines for tippling and other lapses, it is noteworthy that the only expenditure recorded in this book, apart from that on poor relief, is for wine both for communion and for hospitality. At a cost of 2s a bottle and with six bottles needed for Easter and Christmas, on these occasions at least there would be little left in the collection. When the dean of Lincoln, as rector of Chesterfield, made a visit in 1757, two bottles of wine were provided for him and when in August that year Bishop Cornwallis came for a confirmation, the churchwardens spent £1 4s 0d on wine for him, 9s on wine "for his secretary and gentleman" and £1 on their own wine. In this kind of entertainment it seems that the Chesterfield churchwardens conformed to the standards of their time.

Whilst we know something of the customs of religious observance at the parish church from this now lost register, we rely very heavily on the surviving churchwardens accounts and vestry minutes for information on the repairs and alterations to the fabric of the church in this period and for glimpses of other aspects of church life. The main series of churchwardens accounts begin in 1762 but an isolated year's accounts survive for 1744[8]. These, in fact, very much set the pattern for the remainder of the century with little significant change apparent.

The 1744 accounts show the churchwardens entitled to income of just over £96, consisting of £40 from Chesterfield, £40 from the other townships of the parish, £13 6s 4d from rents and £2 from burial fees. The cash actually collected fell short of this total by just over £10, but their expenditure for the year did not exceed £73 so they finished with a surplus of over £13 with a further £5 due from Newbold and Brimington. Almost two-thirds of their payments were to named individuals for unspecified goods and services. The remainder was spent in small sums mostly for routine purposes such as 5s to John Allen for mowing and cleaning the churchyard, 12s for "cleaning the steeple down" and 6s "spent at the repair of the steeple". In addition there were the usual expenses concerned with visitations, communion services and church maintenance, the cost of ringing the bells (£4 5s 0d for eight days), the payment of £1 7s 6d to the singers and finally the wages of the parish church officers. A special feature in this particular year was that with the statement passing the accounts was a declaration, signed by J. Bradley, the mayor, and William Clarke, regulating certain payments in the future. Each churchwarden, for example, was to be allowed £2 at each visitation to be spent at his discretion; also at a visitation the churchwardens of the town were to pay 12d each to the parish clerk, the sexton, the dog whipper and Thomas Hatfield; the singers were not to be paid more than 20s and the annual salary of 26s paid to James Mettam (in what capacity it is not clear) was to cease. Finally, the churchwardens were to be responsible for seeing that the fire engines were kept in good order and that they should be "played" (i.e. tested) twice a year.

At the vestry meeting to which the churchwardens accounts were submitted, some objection was raised to the two payments of 15s paid to John Swift, the collector of window tax, for the vicar's windows. William Wheeler did not insist on this payment as of right but desired that it might continue as had been customary from the time of his predecessor Mr Hinckesman. Wheeler, a Hampshire man and an Oxford graduate, had formerly been curate and schoolmaster at Kimbolton, Huntingdonshire, before coming to Chesterfield as vicar in 1739. Soon after his arrival funds were subscribed to make possible the rebuilding on a larger scale of the north side of the vicarage[9]. According to Pegge, this brought about a great improvement in the house (the "manse") which he could describe as "most commodiously situated...very airy and sufficiently large with all proper conveniences about it". Wheeler's successor, John Wood, vicar from 1765 to 1781 "totally reformed the garden and croft and made it a delightful spot[10].

In 1756[11] during Wheeler's incumbency, there were major alterations to the fabric of the church with the building of the new West Gallery and the installation of a new organ to occupy the East Gallery. John Allwood, Joseph Shipton, Francis Sikes and John Bunting estimated for the West Gallery and contracted to complete the work on or before Midsummer Day 1756 for a price of £130. £638 15s 6d of the £712 5s 6d needed for the work as a whole was raised by subscription and a further £61 9s 0d by the holding of a concert. Mr Snetzler was paid £500 for the organ and £130, as estimated, was paid for the erection of the West Gallery.

Over the years the corporation pews had been improved and it is evident from Samuel Pegge's description of them in the late eighteenth century that they were designed to emphasise the dignity and power of the mayor and corporation, albeit somewhat overstated. The three large and "very noble" seats were able to be extended by a concession from the Hon. Samuel Pierrepont of Thoresby, lord of Calow, of a yard from the Calow seats at the east end of the third seat. According to Pegge, the seats were "very commodiously placed", the first row being reserved for their ladies, the second for the mayor and aldermen, and the third for the town clerk and the six brethren of the corporation. The mayor's seat at the east end was distinguished by a "decent piece of iron work painted and gilt with the king's Arms in proper colours".

The churchwardens accounts from 1762[13] continue in much the same vein as those of 1744. Repairs and maintenance of the fabric, particularly small everyday items, are recited in great detail but little of real moment is recorded. We know that pig fat was used to lubricate the bells, that the occasional hedgehog or fox still penetrated the environs of the church, that the vestry was whitewashed from time to time and that the bells were rung to celebrate the anniversary of the king's coronation for example. One of the few major events in the life of the church to be revealed is that in 1769–1770 extensive repairs were made to the roof and "gable end of the north wall of the cross aisle". One of the few surviving vestry minutes for this period, that of 20 March 1769,refers to the need to raise "twenty leys" for this purpose. The expenditure on this work meant outgoings of over £388 in 1770, rather more than the customary £100–150. Further work on the roof was apparently necessary in 1774 when Francis Moore was paid £218 for such work, a bill surviving in the Pashley Collection[14] to the "entertainment of raising the church roof" in August of that year.

Significant events in church life over the following years are few. Further surgery was carried out on the steeple in 1784 when John Bargh of Barlow inspected it and reported the need for 220 feet of timber and 5 cwts of iron for bolts and screws. In 1788 a new dial was ordered for the clock and the mechanism properly repaired. In June of the same year the vestry ordered that the bells may be rung from 5.45 a.m. to 6.00 a.m. each morning, a practice that would not be popular today. The bells were causing trouble of another sort in 1793, perhaps not wholly unrelated to the above, when it was ordered that one of the bells be recast and the whole put in regular time. In the same year the beadle, Samuel Kirk, was granted an additional salary of 10s per annum for lighting the vestry fires.

Notable occurrences in the everyday life of the church continued to be few in the early years of the nineteenth century. There was sufficient money raised by the church rate assessment of 1807 to add to the church plate, namely two silver communion cups, a silver plate and a large silver dish for receiving alms. The steeple and the bells continued to cause problems: an assessment of sixteen levies was granted in 1810 for work that was needed to render the steeple safe and in 1814 an assessment of six levies was granted for repairing and rehanging the bells. The question of repairs to the steeple reached a climax late in 1817 when independent reports on its state of repair were sought and the general view seemed to be that there was no course of action other than to take it down. W. Wilkinson indeed regarded the spire as "the most ill-designed and ill-constructed mass of confusion I have ever surveyed in my life". E.W. Drury of Sheffield was likewise moved to "recommend that the steeple be taken down to prevent the possibility of an accident"[15]. The sentiments expressed by the surveyors were not sufficient to sway the vestry towards a decision to demolish the town's most notable landmark however, and in 1819 we again find an assessment of eighteen leys being granted for the repair of the steeple. It is interesting that the favourite theory put forward by the surveyors for the warping of the spire at this time was that it was the result of intense heat from the sun shrinking the timbers on the south, south-west and west sides, combined with poor carpentry work. The problem of the bells came to a climax in 1819 when Thomas Meers of the famous Whitechapel Bell Foundry was directed to inspect the bells and he recommended on 28 October 1819 that a complete new peal of ten bells should be acquired instead of continuing to repair the present one. Meers' estimate of £337 3s 4d was accepted. This long episode of repairs to the spire and the bells demonstrates admirably the burden the church was on the ratepayers.

The fire engines continued to cause concern from time to time. In 1799 the vestry was worrying about where to store them. In 1816 they were reported as out of order and as a result of this it was ordered that they should be tested four times a year. Two firemen were also appointed.

In 1822 the formidable Thomas Hill appeared on the scene as vicar of Chesterfield and almost immediately there was a flurry of activity in church affairs. In May 1822 it was decided that it would be expedient to enlarge the churchyard and a series of sales and exchanges of land were proposed. In November of the same year, the propriety of moving the pulpit into the Middle Aisle was being considered. A year later the vestry was considering establishing "a choir of singers" in the church and what compensation should be given to the present occupiers of the singers gallery who would have to vacate their seats. A committee of the vestry determined that £4 should be paid for each of the fifteen sittings in the front

REPORTS

of the State of the Spire of CHESTERFIELD CHURCH.

We whose names are hereunto subscribed did on the 26th November 1817, carefully examine the state of the Wood in the Steeple of Chesterfield Church, and found the Wood not only in a very decayed state in some parts, but the greatest part of the principal timbers having a tendency to push the Steeple towards the South, the top of the steeple is now very far from being perpendicular over its base, which renders it very necessary to prevent the top part of the Steeple going farther Southward. If it be suffered to remain unsupported a few years it will certainly become in a dangerous state, and it is very probable that it will fail at about the Middle of the Steeple and fall towards the South or South West.

D. Hodkin,
B. Tomlinson.

After a careful and minute examination of the timbers and their respective bearings to each other, I feel justified in drawing the following conclusions.

The principal timbers on the South, South West, and West sides of the Spire, I found in a very decayed state, and many of the original Rafters out of their perpendicular direction, as much as one foot in six, inclining to one side, and several of those above them incline nearly as much the contrary way, which shews that the connection of those timbers is completely disjointed and broken, and consequently their perpendicular bearing is destroyed; I likewise found several diagonal pieces of timber counteracting the intention for which they were originally introduced, as instead of supporting the hollow side which is giving way, they are supporting the round side, and making it rounder still to the North, North East and East.

Many of the original timbers are broken, some through rottenness and large knots, and from an over and irregular pressure, others are quite loose, and consequently of no use, and one large piece I found had dropped from its original position, which lay upon the floor below.

When I was in the Crow Hole near the top, in looking out at the door I was surprised to observe myself considerably over the perpendicular of the Base towards the South; I conceive it could not be less than *six feet*. I therefore should imagine (but which I had not an opportunity of observing minutely on account of the rain) that the point of the spire is nearly *eight feet* out of its perpendicular direction; the idea of its giving way much further struck me with terror, at what *might be* the consequence, should it fall suddenly during the time of Divine Service, as it would certainly fall on the main body of the Church.

The general principle of its construction as a piece of Carpenter's Work is very bad and injudicious, and such as would disgrace the most inexperienced Carpenter of the present age; but I have observed this to be the case in most pieces of Ancient Carpenter's Work I have examined in different parts of the Kingdom.

Some of the strong upright timbers in the interior are decayed, and in some places broken, and have been patched by means of planks screwed to the sides, some of which are fastened to the rotten parts, and of course useless. I am well aware that a considerable expence has been from time to time incurred by these means, and to very little purpose; in short it is the most ill designed and ill constructed mass of confusion I ever surveyed in my life, for a work of such magnitude.

I feel the fullest confidence that the angles originally pointed directly towards the Weathercock from the Base, but in consequence of the original Rafters swerving from their position, that screw like present appearance has been produced; and I think it probable that the Sun's intense heat having shrunk the timbers on the three sides the most exposed thereto, has in some degree contributed to the state in which I found it; and this cause will continue till the steeple is no more. Indeed I have invariably observed that even stone spires have been considerably more out of repair on the South, South West, and West Sides, than the others; and this I can only attribute to the Sun's strong influence thereon.

From all these considerations, and from the difficulty I find in introducing new standards in a proper position so as to make a permanent repair, (the unsightly and dangerous appearance of which cannot by any means be improved) independent of the vast expence that would be necessary, I am of opinion that the most effectual, and ultimately the most safe and economical way will be, to take down the whole of the spire, and substitute something in its stead of a more durable nature, more especially as the Timber and Lead might probably go towards such as would be required to furnish a handsome, respectable, and appropriate stone termination above the square part of the tower, which is in its [illegible].

Wood House, Mansfield, Dec. 19, 1817.

W. Wilkinson.

To the Churchwardens of the Parish Church of Chesterfield.

GENTLEMEN,

Agreeable to the request of Mr [illegible], I attended on Monday the [illegible] of December instant, to inspect the Steeple of your Church, and am quite of opinion that it is unsafe and dangerous to remain in its present state; for on inspection I found the Old Timber much decayed, and the construction of the whole so imperfect, that it would be impossible to repair it, even at any expence, so as to ensure its standing many years; being extremely weakened by its being so much out of plumb to the South, from the Tower to the Centre, and to the West from its Centre upwards.

I should therefore recommend that the Steeple be taken down to prevent the possibility of an accident, the event of which would inevitably do considerable damage to the Roof and Body of the Church, and erect on the Tower which is strong and sufficient, a Stone Steeple.

I am Gentlemen,

Your most obedient Servant,

Sheffield 20th Dec. 1817. *E. W. Drury.*

A VESTRY MEETING

will be held on Thursday the 29th Inst. at 11 o'Clock in the Forenoon, to take the above Reports into consideration,

January 3, 1818.

(BRADLEY, PRINTER, CHESTERFIELD.)

Notice of a vestry meeting to discuss the future of the spire, 29 December 1817

two rows of the gallery. In 1824 the question of enlarging the churchyard was taken a stage further with the drawing up of plans and the not unreasonable decision to ban washing lines from it. The Duke of Devonshire agreed to sell land on the north side to the parish church for £350 and to finance this three church properties in the town were to be sold. The efforts to stop children playing, hanging of washing lines and other nuisances were apparently unsuccessful, for in 1831 a decision was taken to enclose the churchyard.

Archdeacon Butler's parochial visitation[16] took place in 1823–4, the early years of Hill's incumbency, and provides a more than useful summary of the state of the parish church at that time. Overall a fairly healthy picture is painted of the church and its services, the most serious compaints being about the drains in the churchyard which "do mischief" and the church clock which may have been repaired in 1788 but was described as "very old and indifferent". The lack of accommodation for the poor was commented on, a problem to which Hill was to devote much attention. The spire was described as "twisted and very curious"and compared to Dijon in France but was said to be "in repair". The vicarage was referred to as "a large old house with three sitting rooms, six bedrooms, servants rooms and suitable offices". The need to increase the size of the churchyard was stressed reflecting the attention being paid to the subject by the vestry.

Sunday services in 1823–4 consisted of a sermon in the morning, a lecture in the evening and an additional service in the evening for the benefit of the poor. Prayers were held on Wednesdays and Fridays and the average number of communicants was said to be 50, a number much augmented at Easter.

In 1825 there was a foretaste of the great repewing saga of the 1840s (see Vol.III *Early Victorian Chesterfield* Chapter 8) when it was decided to ask Mr Hodkin to draw up a plan and survey for improving the church interior and enlarging the accommodation. Mr Lucas and Mr Harwood were appointed to superintend this work. The plan ran into immediate opposition from pew owners however, and the long story of the vicar's fight to repew and restore the church had effectively begun.

Nonconformity in Chesterfield 1660–1835

In the return of dissenting places of worship to Derbyshire Quarter Sessions in 1829[17] some 1408 people were recorded as being Protestant dissenters. It would be wrong to interpret this as a precise figure as presumably this was intended to represent the general order of congregations in the various denominations, but it seems to represent around one quarter of the population of the borough (5775 in 1831). Bishop Compton's "census" of 1676[18] had recorded 100 Protestant Nonconformists out of an adult population for the parish of 3500. It would be wrong to read too much into either figure in absolute terms but it does indicate a substantial element of Protestant dissent in the town both at the beginning and the end of the period with the advent of Methodism after 1780 emphasising the point.

Much of the earliest evidence of nonconformity in the town concerns the Quakers but there are also allusions to people with puritan sympathies within the established church before the Civil Wars. The life of John Shaw, a well-known preacher in Yorkshire in the middle decades of the seventeenth century, provides some insight into this subject[19]. A native of Bradfield and a graduate of Cambridge, where he was a contemporary of John Milton at Christ's College, Shaw's first appointment was as curate at Brampton in 1630, where he says "I continued lecturer for three years, there being at that time only one, Mr Wood (commonly called a reading-minister) there". Shortly after moving to Brampton Shaw was licenced to preach by the Bishop of Coventry and Lichfield, as Mr Wood had evidently not qualified for such a licence.

In 1632 Shaw married Dorothy, eldest daughter of George and Dorothy Heathcote of Cutthorpe Hall, Brampton, at York. Dorothy appears to have been a woman of exceptional virtue and religious zeal. In one tribute after her death in Hull Nicholas Heathcote wrote, "I remember her constantly coming every lord's day from Cutthorp-hall to Chesterfield (which was two good miles) to partake of worthy Mr Wainwright's ministry[20] and was neither detained by the scorching heat in summer, nor yet deterred by the coldnesse of the winter". John Shaw described more fully her family life at Cutthorpe, the pattern of which was set by the religious attitudes of her parents, who encouraged her early religious interests through bible reading and "good sermon books" and the discussion of sermons. Of greater interest however, is his fuller account of her visits to Chesterfield, made because of her dissatisfaction with the reading-minister at Brampton. On these occasions, after hearing "a faithful preacher", Shaw describes how she "instead of her dinner, went to a private house, where many godly persons used to meet, where the sermon was repeated, and other duties performed, and so again to the publick ordinance in the afternoon, and so home at night". Such gatherings played a crucial part in the development of puritan ideas and attitudes at this time. By their nature, they have left few records and it is very fortunate that from the life of John Shaw there is this significant glimpse in the 1630s of this group within the church meeting in a private house to advance their religious purposes. John Shaw left Brampton after three years for Chumleigh in Devon, but after a similar period returned to Yorkshire were he established a notable reputation as a preacher in York, Rotherham and Hull until his career was curtailed by the Act of Uniformity in 1662.

Three other ministers deprived of their livings by the Act of Uniformity were linked with religious life in Chesterfield. Joseph Swetnam seceded from his curacy of All Saints, Derby, before the act was applied. Since he had become rector of Dalbury in 1624, he had held a number of offices in the county. In the 1650s he was known for his royalist views, a newsletter, 30 May 1653, saying "the Presbyterians speak out boldly for the king e.g. Mr Swetnam of Derby". On 13 January 1659/60 there is an enigmatic reference to his compounding for the first fruits on his admission to the vicarage of Chesterfield, but there is no evidence that he ever took possession of the living.

John Wood was the son of Richard Wood, an influential druggist in Chesterfield, churchwarden in 1636. From the grammar school he went in 1651 to St Johns College, Cambridge, where he became a Fellow seven years later, but was deprived of this office in 1662. He preached in Derbyshire "In several churches, reading much of the Common Prayer: But he us'd to say he did not like subscribing to Conformity"[21]. In 1672 he was licenced as a Presbyterian preacher at his house at Norton, possibly Nether Norton Hall, which his father had bought in 1651. He married a sister of Robert Fern who was the first minister at the Elder Yard Chapel with Thomas Ogle.

Another minister in Chesterfield who was unable to conform to the Act of Uniformity was John Ford, the son of an alderman and mayor of the town. He had entered Magdelene College, Cambridge, at the age of eighteen in 1651 and after graduating had returned to Chesterfield, probably assisting Billingsley for whom he is known to have had the greatest respect although not sharing his Presbyterian beliefs[22]. A sketch of Ford is given by Calamy:[23]

> "of a melancholy Temper and much inclin'd to Silence; but his Silence was not unfruitful; for his few words were usually full of Worth and Weight. He needed much entreaty to be brought to his Preaching-Work; but when he was engag'd he made amends to those who had bestow'd pains to persuade him. He was Congregational in his Judgment. . ."

He died before reaching the age of thirty "spent by severe study".

Derbyshire has many links with the formative years of the Quaker movement. It was one of the counties in which George Fox, the founder of the movement, first raised his voice, and it was in Derby in 1650 that he and his followers were first called Quakers by one of the justices, Gervase Bennett, who imprisoned him in the House of Correction there. He had travelled to Derby from Chesterfield where he had suffered the same penalty. In his *Journal*[24], Fox describes his meeting with Thomas Bretland, then the lecturer in Chesterfield who "saw beyond the common sort of priests, for he had been partly convinced . . . but when the priest of that town died, he got the parsonage and choked himself with it". However, Bretland and others to whom Fox addressed himself took him before the mayor and he was sent to the House of Correction. His imprisonment in Chesterfield was very brief for, as Fox said, "in the night the officers, with the watchmen, put me out of the town, leaving us to shift as we could."

His visit was not, however, without influence it would seem, for the following year Col. Edmundson, whose troops were stationed in Chesterfield, reported that in the town "the common discourse of all sorts of people was of the Quakers". Strange stories were told against them, but he himself was drawn to them after hearing two women preach in the Market Place; they had been abused by a clergyman and a young merchant, who was with Edmundson, called his action "a poor victory over two defenceless women". Subsequently Edmundson was convinced by James Naylor and himself undertook Quaker missionary work in Ireland[25].

The most famous of the early Derbyshire Quakers was John Gratton who was born at Bakewell in 1642 and whose life and especially his religious experiences are recorded in his *Journal*[26]. Before he became a Quaker he had sought to find religious satisfaction with other sects. Discontented with the Presbyterians, he went Chesterfield to meet the Independents but despite some liking for them he judged them to be "dead professors and dry trees, not bringing forth fruit" and moreover he scorned the strict precautions taken to keep their meetings secret. It was in Chesterfield also that he read, and rejected as false, the book which inspired the Muggletonians. He became a Quaker in 1664 and from 1668 until his death in 1711 he lived at Monyash, the village with which he is always most closely associated. From there he travelled to preach in many parts of Derbyshire and neighbouring counties, his defiance of the Conventicle Acts leading amongst other things to imprisonment in the House of Correction at Derby and in 1676 to a fine of £20 in Chesterfield. This latter punishment arose from a meeting he attended at Whittington in the house of Francis Davenport, a milliner. The mayor of Chesterfield, Richard Clarke, was also there, as were two informers sent by the vicar. Clarke was interested in, and strangely moved by, Gratton's preaching "though poor soul he was very rich in worldly riches, and it was too hard for him to stand in a publick profession of the truth with us". Despite the sympathy of the mayor, Gratton was fined and Francis Davenport's cattle and horses were sold by order of a Dronfield magistrate for the payment of the same fine of £20. In his later years Gratton was a frequent visitor to Chesterfield and to the meetings at Tupton.

The first Quakers that can be identified in the Chesterfield area are John Frith, Thomas Brocksopp and Anthony Wright[27]. Frith

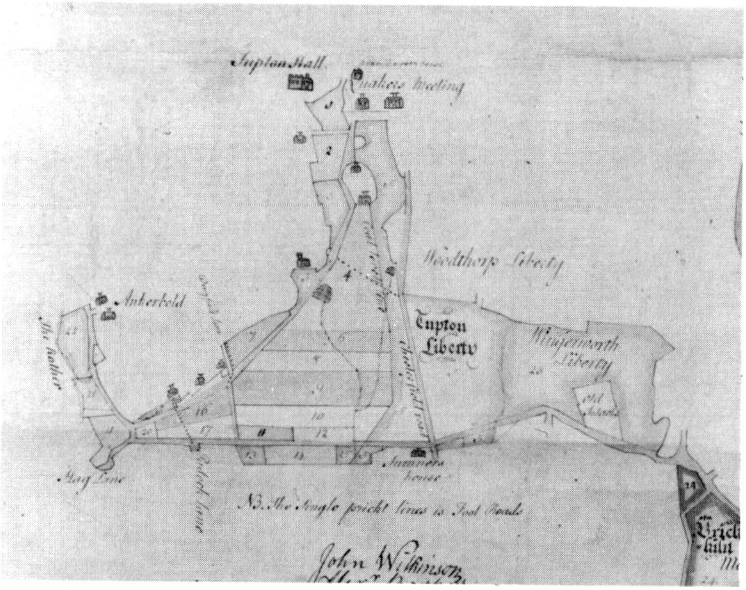

Part of the plan accompanying the Wingerworth enclosure award of 1758 showing the position of the Friends Meeting House in Tupton

had a horse taken away from him in 1657 for a refusal to pay 3s tithe rent and Easter offerings, whilst Brocksopp and Wright of Whittington and Brampton respectively were imprisoned for refusing to remove their hats before magistrates. Such punishments continued after the Restoration. In 1663, fifteen who had been arrested at illegal meetings were kept in the House of Correction in Chesterfield for terms ranging from three to nine weeks[28]. Two years later the four leaders of the Quaker meeting of the town, Susannah Frith, John Allen, William Storrs and Elizabeth Holmes, were sent to the House of Correction

During the 1660s pressure on the Quakers under the Conventicle Acts increased, particularly by the increase in fines. In one year for instance, William Storrs, a member of one of the town's leading Quaker families, who were involved in the lead trade, paid fines amounting to £75. The Quakers thrived on persecution, however, and it has been estimated that numbers in the country doubled to about 70,000 and the movement may well have reached its peak about 1680[29].

This growth was reflected in the development of the Quakers' local organisation. In 1672 a quarterly meeting was instituted in Derbyshire, with the earliest meetings in the Chesterfield district being held at Tupton Moor in a house "purchased by the general charge". It is thought likely to be the house at the entrance to what is now Tupton Hall School[30]. Other meetings were held at two farmhouses on the moors near Chesterfield, Peasunhurst and Buntingfield, both in the parish of Ashover, owned by a noted Quaker family called Booth. Early Quaker burial grounds are recorded both at Tupton and Peasunhurst. In 1685 one meeting was held in Joshua Arnold's house at Boythorpe but it was not until 1692 that a quarterly meeting was recorded in Chesterfield itself at the "Old Hall", a house occupied by Thomas Burbeck but not yet identified with certainty. It was one of the four meeting houses registered for Quaker worship in Chesterfield under the terms of the Toleration Act of 1689. The others were owned by John Frith, Godfrey Tomlinson and Joseph Frith[31]. John Frith, dyer, had been among a list of Chesterfield Quakers presented by the constable of Chesterfield to Quarter Sessions in 1683; the others were Peter Parkinson, woollen draper, and Ann his wife, Laurence Oxley, lead merchant and his wife, Thomas Burbeck, dyer, and Elizabeth his wife, Susannah Frith, widow, and William Storrs, woollen draper. The tendency for leading tradesmen to be Quakers is already very apparent from this list[32].

The next step, agreed upon at a Tupton meeting in 1695, was to build a meeting house in Chesterfield. In April 1696 it was agreed that William Storrs should loan the money required for the building and that seven Friends – Richard Clayton, Joshua Arnold, John Bower, Joseph Holland, Anthony Haslam, Godfrey Beard and Philip Maden – should form a committee to find a suitable site[33]. This was found on Saltergate and early in 1697 Joshua Arnold was authorised to buy the necessary building materials and to engage workmen and William Storrs to receive and disburse the contributions promised by Friends. The building was ready to be used for the first meeting on 28 October 1697: it had cost £70 and contributions were sought from meetings throughout the county. The meeting house in Saltergate was a simple largely brick building with three stone-headed sash windows and a plain door. Old stone rubble was used for one side wall. The interior was also characteristically simple and undemonstrative, half being open to the full height of the building and half divided into two floors to give the customary gallery of a Quaker meeting house. It was demolished to make way for the Saltergate multi-storey car park.

The records of the early quarterly and monthly meetings throw interesting light on the Quaker way of life. The relief of the poor and sick was a primary responsibility, rents from property at Newbold, Ashover and elsewhere being used together with money from collections and legacies to provide small pensions, often 4s a month, for poor and aged Quakers. Other payments were made to those in prison or suffering misfortunes like fire. Loans were often made, sometimes possibly for business reasons, and their repay-

The Friends Meeting House, Saltergate

ment regularly recorded. An early and pleasant example of this practice occured in 1674 when Robert Dawson, possibly the butcher whose inventory in 1698 showed his personal possessions to be worth £18 19s 0d, "brought in twenty shillings of the money that was lent him by Friends, being in all thirty shillings, so friends gave him five shillings back and forgave the ten shillings that was behind". The funds of the quarterly meeting were also used to apprentice boys and girls to Quakers: for example, in 1677 when William Jones of Ashover apprenticed his daughter to Hercules Harvey of Chesterfield for seven years "to learn the art of holeing and stitching bodices", the meeting contributed £3.

From 1674 the records show the strict supervision exercised over Quaker marriages. In 1705 Thomas Harvey had "taken up with some unworthy person" so Joseph Frith and John Storrs were delegated to speak with him and shortly afterwards he found a more satisfactory partner. When the mother of Barbara Heathcote of Loads objected to her proposed marriage to William Pyke of London, the matter was investigated and then, after a considerable delay, the marriage approved. The desire of John Bower of Chander Hill to marry Alice Booth of Peasunhurst, a widow, was similarly approved but only after suitable provision had been made for her children. Inevitably difficulties did arise and marriages were opposed: in 1684 that proposed between Joshua Arnold and Anne Higgins was forbidden because he was "unfaithful to God and she unconvinced of the Truth". Historically the most interesting of these Quaker marriages in Chesterfield was that between Mary Storrs and John Fry, whose son Joseph was the founder of the chocolate firm.

More generally, the personal conduct of Quakers was of direct concern to the meeting and the regular enquiries made must have had considerable influence in firmly establishing the distinctive Quaker way of life. Those falling below the required standards of behaviour were invited to explain their failings to the meeting and were often admonished, occasionally disowned. A typical case was that of Joseph Gratton in 1707 who was reprimanded for his disorderly conduct, strong drink and careless trading and then promised to reform. In the same year Jeffrey Asher was disowned for "overshooting himself in debt and not making his condition known", but was later reinstated. Some tendencies to revert to the practices of the established church were checked:Andrew Gillon and his wife were rebuked in 1709 for having their child "sprinkled": William Walker rather curiously sought to justify his attendance at church by saying that unless he did his children would be ruined and in any case many honest people went to church; and in 1716 Joseph Cowley undertook to remove a gravestone as "a needless and superstitious practice". A number of Quakers were disowned for being married by a priest. Not all however were so submissive: two women persisted in the seemingly common custom of "disorderly walking" and David Maltby, who had been censured for marrying his maidservant, rejected this intrusion into his private life.

Such failings may be indicative of the more relaxed atmosphere in religious movements as the spirit of enthusiasm and persecution of the seventeenth century receded. The growth of toleration was accompanied by some decline in the intensity of religious feeling which had its effect on the Quaker movement. A regular theme in the meeting records is the slackening of activity, often expressed in a failure to make what were considered to be adequate subscriptions and falling attendances. As early as the 1690s money for the new meeting house at Chesterfield was collected slowly and by 1714 it was being proposed that because of smaller numbers at Tupton, the monthly meetings should be moved to Chesterfield, as indeed they soon were. These problems became more serious and in 1729 Stephen Arnold was given the task of remonstrating with the local Quakers about the state of their subscriptions. For years the persistent slackness in attendance at the women's monthly meetings was being deplored and reference made to "a drowsy disposition that is too apt to prevail in some of our meetings".

To turn from the Quakers to the Presbyterian and Independent dissenters[34], for some thirty-two years after the ejection of the Presbyterian John Billingsley from the incumbency of the parish church in 1662, they had no place of worship other than private houses. Under the Declaration of Indulgence of 1672 five private houses were licenced as "conventicles" in which worship could take place, three of them Independent – the houses of George Poynton, Thomas Ogle and George White – and the other two Presbyterian – Peter Parkinson and John Bromily.

The Toleration Act of 1689 enabled Protestant dissenters for the first time to build their own chapels or meeting houses and the initiative to provide an Independent Chapel was taken by Cornelius Clarke of Norton, an influential person in the late seventeenth century town. Because of the complexity of the Clarke pedigrees he has on occasion been described at the son of Ralph Clarke who was the first mayor of Chesterfield in 1598. His father was in fact also Ralph Clarke but son of Ralph Clarke the first mayor. Ralph II was also mayor on several occasions but achieved greatest prominence as a leading Parlimentarian in Derbyshire during the Civil Wars and Republican period. Cornelius (1631–1696) came to manhood therefore, when Puritanism was in the ascendant. He served as justice of the peace from 1665 to 1671 but not again until 1689, a significant break pointing to his dissent from prevailing political and religious policies. In 1669 he had been high sheriff of Derbyshire very soon after he had bought the manor and other estates at Norton from the trustees of William Bullock, a Royalist whose fortunes had not recovered from the losses arising from the Civil Wars before his death in 1666.

The Clarkes by contrast had undoubtedly gained in wealth during the interregnum as is shown by the inclusion of Cornelius in a list of Derbyshire gentry drawn up in 1662, two years after the death of his father[35]. He is included in the group, mostly lead merchants, who had not served the king but who were considered "fit persons to lend the king money". His annual income was estimated at £500 and his personal wealth at £6000. From this time he was extending his financial influence over the Norton estate, the acquisition of which gave him a position among landed families more commensurate with his riches than had his father's more modest property at Cutthorpe.

On 26 October 1692, Cornelius Clarke purchased from John Smith, hatter, "a parcel of land in or near to a place called Ellar Yard", meaning "elder tree enclosure", being part of a croft formerly belonging to Humphrey Petty and in area 40 by 23 yards. His intention was to erect on this plot a building which was to serve as "a place of meeting for dissenting protestants for religious worship". This was completed in 1694 and on 17 April of that year registered at the Quarter Sessions in Derby. The cost of the land and the building, according to Ford, was £229 10s 0d. Cornelius Clarke also acquired a strip of land about 80 yards long and 2–3 yards wide to provide a way to the meeting house. By 1695 the land and the building were vested in six trustees[36]; the deed included a provision that if Nonconformist ministers or preachers were ever to be maintained or preferred in the same way as ministers of the established church, the property should be held by the trustees to the use of Cornelius Clarke and his heirs. Future ministers were to be chosen by "the greater number of the usual auditors, being housekeepers", and such appointments were to be for life. Finally, Cornelius Clarke, who died in 1696, left £80 in his will for the purchase of a suitable house or manse for the minister, provided that the congregation would raise a sufficient sum to supplement this bequest. A house with land was bought in 1697 for £100 from Robert Mower of Barlow Woodseats. According to the deed, this was located in St Mary's Gate on the south side of its junction with Spital (or Hollis) Lane, the site in part now occupied by the Old Ship Inn[36].

The fabric of the meeting house of 1694 remains today without substantial change, but the usual view from the modern Elder Way may be misleading as it is the western end and not the front which faces the street. The south-facing front has to be approached through the burial ground which is largely hidden from the street to form an unexpected enclosure with trees in the centre of the town. This original front has a wide central bay projecting slightly under a pediment with a small round window. The main doorway

Elder Yard Chapel

in the centre has a segmental pediment with a panel in the frieze and above another panel recording the date of the building in a rusticated surround. The central bay and the bays on either side have quoins and four windows with stone mullions and transoms in which some of the small panes of original glass have been preserved. The walls are now rough-cast but the stonework may originally have been exposed. The main front was extended by the plain bay at the east end when the chancel was built in 1821.

The interior, some 50 by 25 feet, has undergone more changes but nevertheless retains a number of interesting original features. The present pulpit probably stood at the centre of the north wall facing the south doorway; it then had a sounding board and would have been higher just as the box pews were higher than the present ones. At the west end was the gallery one pillar of which still has painted on it the date of 1694 and the names of two members of the congregation, Mellor Pade and Edward Turner. The pulpit, pews and gallery, largely in oak, are plain style and good in quality. They contribute effectively to the quiet dignity which appropriately characterises this early meeting house for worship by Protestant dissenters.

A point of special interest in the early years of the chapel was its joint use by Presbyterians and Independents or Congregationalists, the two main strands of the puritan movement in the Civil Wars fifty years earlier, which drew apart in the Commonwealth but which had been brought together again by their common deprivation of religious freedoms after the restoration of the monarchy and church in 1660. Indeed, there has been some uncertainty about the exact allegiance of the first two ministers who officiated at the chapel from its opening until 1703. The older man, Thomas Ogle, had been in Chesterfield since at least 1672 and seems to have been in Calamy's words "congregational in his judgment". The suggestion made in Ford's *History*[37] that he was Presbyterian and related to Cornelius Clarke no doubt arises from his marriage to Lydia, Clarke's sister, and the widow of George Heathcote of Cutthorpe[38]. The other minister, Robert Ferne, a Presbyterian, was, like Ogle, one of the first dissenting preachers to be licenced in Derbyshire in 1689. In that year the list of registered meeting houses includes one at Norton Lees with Robert Ferne as the owner, and in Chesterfield the owner of one such house was Robert Ferne[39]. His sister had married John Wood, the Presbyterian minister at Norton, so both ministers had links through marriage with that strong centre of the sect. Not surprisingly, he also had contact with the most famous of Presbyterian preachers in Derbyshire, William Bagshawe of Ford Hall, commonly known as "the apostle of the Peak". In the latter's journal[40], for instance, there is a record of a conference at Ashford when Robert Ferne and other ministers "spoke largely" on temperance.

Soresby Street Independent Chapel

It is from William Bagshawe's life that we know of the existence of a presbytery in Chesterfield in 1651, for it was here before "a very numerous" assembly that he was ordained, the moderator at that time being Immanuel Bourne, the rector of Ashover. Ferne remained in Chesterfield until 1703 when he moved to Wirksworth, where he died in 1727 at the age of seventy-five.

The joint use of the chapel by Presbyterians and Congregationalists had been cemented in 1703 by the drawing up of an agreement in November by which each party was allowed to elect its own minister and each party was represented by an equal number of trustees. The two ministers were also allowed to occupy the house. The agreement appears to have lasted until 1721 after which date there were no more Congregational ministers at Elder Yard: the Congregationalist congregation seems to have remained associated with the chapel for a further fifty years or so although the ministers were all Presbyterian.

The Congregationalists withdrew during the period in which the Rev. Thomas Astley was minister (from 1773), first moving to the Blue Meeting House in Froggatt's Yard, off New Square (1778), and subsequently to the Rose Hill Independent Chapel (1822). The reason for the split appears to have been Astley's Unitarian leanings which became more apparent during his ministry and culminated in the chapel becoming known as the Unitarian Chapel by 1818, a year after Astley's death. Astley had also kept a school in Chesterfield up to around 1800 and was also responsible for starting a vestry library. The Sunday School started in 1813 around the time of his retirement and it is interesting to note several tradesmen – Robert Malkin, Robert Woodhead and Henry Malkin, for instance – among the twelve members of the congregation who were signatories to the statement founding the Sunday School.

Astley's successor as minister was the Rev. George Kendrick but he was soon succeeded in 1815 by the Rev. Robert Wallace from Manchester College. During his ministry the first changes to the fabric referred to earlier took place and in 1828 land fronting Saltergate to the east of the chapel was acquired by exchange with the Duke of Devonshire for building schools. The first school buildings were erected in 1831 with Boys and Girls Schools arranged each side of a central entrance. The Independent Chapel of 1697 was indeed flourishing as the Unitarian Chapel by 1830, the 1829 return of dissenting places of worship recording the congregation as 250, only slightly smaller than the Congregational figure.

By the 1820s however, all the other Nonconformist sects had been eclipsed by the Methodists who in the 1829 return claimed 750 adherents, as against 658 for all the other churches combined. Methodism had reached Chesterfield on Wednesday 17 July 1776[41] when John Wesley rode into the town in response to an invitation from local sympathisers after preaching at Doncaster and Sheffield on the previous days. These people failed to meet him in the event, but undeterred he preached to a congregation from the steps at the top of the Market Place. He paid a second visit a year later and again preached from the same vantage point to a large congregation. In 1781 Benjamin Wilkinson from the Sheffield Circuit made two attempts to preach in the town: on his second attempt, on Spital Green, his safety was endangered when he was pelted with missiles. A few years later, Mr Ingle from Brimington – where the local congregation had joined the Sheffield Plan – began a service in the Market Place. He was arrested and taken to the mayor who released him on condition that he obtained a room in the Independents' Blue Meeting House in Froggatt's Yard on the south side of the Market Place. The Methodists made use of this accommodation for a short time and then moved into a room off Packers Row. It was not until 1795 therefore, that the Wesleyan Methodist Chapel on Saltergate was built, being considerably enlarged in 1822. As the movement gained strength, the Chesterfield Wesleyan Methodist Circuit was formed in 1806, with Wesleyan chapels being built at Brampton and Whittington by 1835.

A group of Primitive Methodists held their first class in the town in 1810 and their first conference in 1820. For a time they met in a cottage in Froggatt's Yard. A Primitive Methodist Circuit was formed two years later but no chapel was built within the borough boundaries until 1848: the Brampton Mount Zion Chapel was built in 1827 and a year later a Primitive Methodist Chapel was built at Whittington.

It was not unusual for churches built by Nonconformist sects in the early years of the nineteenth century to change hands several times, perhaps as the majority of the congregation changed its allegiance to another sect under the influence of an individual preacher. The early years of the Baptist church in the town appear to have been far from stable, Ford reporting that the Baptists' meeting house in South Place had fallen into the hands of the Arminian Methodists in 1833[42]. The small Baptist congregation of the opening decades of the century had originated as an offshoot of the Sheffield Baptists with the church being formed on 3 August 1817 when Mr Moreton of Sheffield baptised two persons in a "river adjoining the town", presumably the Hipper. The meeting house was enlarged in 1821 but there were soon problems in raising sufficient funds to provide for a permanent minister, hence its closure and transfer to a Methodist sect.

Saltergate Methodist Chapel

SOME CONCLUDING THOUGHTS

In contrast to the period of rapid institutional change between 1837 and 1850, the period between the Restoration and the accession of Victoria is one of almost complete inertia. The various bodies involved in running the town's affairs were unchanged throughout the period and their positions relative to each other were maintained. The unreformed borough contributed little to the everyday running of the town and even less to its services. Such public services as there were continued to be provided through the vestry and the manor, and it is only in the 1820s that one can detect the beginnings of change with the corporation involvement in the provision of the first gas lighting and piped water. The continued division of functions between the various bodies perhaps makes more sense when it is realised that, to some extent, the same group of people were involved. It should also be remembered that, whilst the corporation as a whole contributed little, the personal power of the mayor was immense: by virtue of being mayor he had a pre-eminent position in all the instruments of government, as the town's justice of the peace, chairman of the vestry, foreman of the jury of the manor court, as well as being mayor.

Whilst there was the stillstand in the institutional structure, the town itself was slowly changing. From the mid eighteenth century population was increasing steadily and towards the end of the period, rapidly, putting a strain on the archaic institutions, and putting a strain on space in the central area. The basic pattern of economic activity remained remarkably stable with heavy industry kept at bay outside the borough boundaries and small-scale workshop and craft industries continued to predominate. The market and its attendant services continued to dominate the town and to outsiders it was the market that seemed to symbolise the town. Nevertheless, some changes were apparent and the town did not escape completely the changes associated with the Industrial Revolution period so apparent elsewhere. Some industries came and went and in the eighteenth century the factory came to

Chesterfield in the form of Tucker's silk mill although, in keeping with the general air of inertia, it did not herald any great wave of factory development. The canal brought cheap water transport up to the edge of the borough but, again, its significance was greater to the mineral-based industries of the hinterland than to the ancient core of the borough itself.

In religious life change was more apparent with a continually changing pattern of dissenting worship over the period. There was always a strong element of religious dissent in the town and throughout the period the established church was under threat from many directions. In the early days the Quakers and the Independents were the chief form of dissent: from the 1780s there was the great surge of Methodism and the appearance of the Unitarian and Baptist congregations.

The Chesterfield of 1830 was a rather cramped, increasingly overcrowded market town, dominated by its market and traditional industry, ruled by a combination of increasingly archaic institutions coming under growing pressure from a changing world. The following decades witnessed a belated response to this changing world: that is the story of the early Victorian era.

APPENDICES

Appendix A Transcript of DRO,D267,C7.

The Accompts of John Ashe and William Dowker Chamberlaines to Mr Richard Clarke late Mayor for one whole yeare ended at Michaelmas Last 1678 made examined & ye . . . day of . . . 167.

Their charge is as followeth	li	s	d
Received of the precedent Chamberlaine Francis Holdesworth Corporacon Stocke	61	10	09
Brackenfield Annuity	12	00	00
Ashover rents	27	06	08
Corporacon rents			
Widdow East house & Booth house	05	06	08
Samuel Farrand for the Tenters	00	07	00
Tho:Ludlam for the garden	00	02	06
William Lee for shopp under the Hall	00	13	04
Tho:Granger for the Gate house	00	05	00
William Beatson for his shopp under ye hall	00	08	00
Benjamin Heathcote for his house	05	06	08
Tho:Marryott for a Shopp in ye Butchery	01	10	00
Mr Gilbert Heathcote for Boythorpe Closes	03	10	00
Mr Fra:Webster for Corporacon land	07	10	00
Widd:Gryme for shopp under the Hall	00	06	08
Tho: Potts for Corporacon lands	02	00	00
Mr Richard Clarke for Cockpitt yard	02	12	00
Edward Needham for Horse Mill and Cockpit house	02	00	00
Carlton rent	05	00	00
Of William Thorpe late Constable being money paid to the Clerke of the Peace for comeing hither at Mr Mayors takeing the oathes	02	03	03
Of Mr Spencer 10^{li} Lingards money	10	00	00
Cutting money for the whole yeare	01	17	04
Of William Beatson for his burgesse fine	00	10	00
Interest of 200^{li} lords money	10	00	00
Interest of 10^{li} Mr Bretlands legacy	00	10	00
Received of Tho:Dutton	02	01	05
Of John Osland spoone money for Robert Wright	00	12	00
Of Mr Alderman Dowker of Lingards money	02	10	00
Of the Churchwardens Anth: Woodwards rent	00	13	04
	168	12	07

Allowances and disbursements

The said Accomptants crave allowance as followeth

	li	s	d
Paid to the Clerke of the Peace when Mr Mayor tooke the oathes at the Sessions	02	00	00
Paid to Mr Mayor as appeares by his Bill for a horse to Welbeck & spent	02	06	08
Paid Widdow Greaves for bread	05	04	00
Paid the overseers of the Poore of Chesterfield	06	16	06
Paid the Towne Clerke to Lent Assize	00	10	00
Paid Mr Spencer one yeares Sallary	03	00	00
for hearth money for the New house	00	02	00
Paid Mr Mayor to Lent Assize	00	10	00
Paid Mr Mayor to Midsummer Assize	00	10	00
Paid Mr Tho: Dowker 10li Lingards money which was received of Mr Spencer	10	00	00
Paid the said Mr Dowker Mr Woodward & Mr Youle which was received of Mr Alderman Dowker	02	10	00
Paid the overseers of Normanton	00	03	06
Paid Fra:Browne & Henry Booth overseers of the Poore of Chesterfield	06	16	08
Paid Anthony Woodward for Ringinge	00	15	00
Paid Mr Mayor his Allowance	10	00	00
Paid the overseers of the Poore for the interest of 200li Lords money	10	00	00
Paid them the interest of 10li Mr Bretlands legacye	00	10	00
Paid for Sacke for Mr Mayor & the Company at Alice Ashes	00	04	00
To Job Brundley for a new Common Prayer Booke	01	12	06
To the overseers of the Poore of Brampton	04	11	00
overseers of Wingerworth	02	05	06
overseers of Hasland	01	11	00
overseers of Newbould	02	03	08
overseers of Calowe	01	01	00
overseers of Normanton	00	07	00
To Mr Foliambe for Antho: Woodwards rent	00	13	04
To Mr Kitchin the rent of the Townes Hall	00	10	00
To William Worrall for repaireing the house of . . .	00	01	06
To Godfrey Clayton for goeing to Ashover	00	00	06
	78	01	00

Allowances & disbursements

To Tho: Salt for a lock & a band for bowleing Greene doore	00	01	06
To James Lambert for the dyehouse	00	06	08
To the Towne Clerke his Sallary	06	00	00
& for writeing as appeares by his bill	00	13	06
Paid Mr Coope for a Sermon	01	00	00
for a Veale & a Mutton to Welbecke	02	05	00
for the hire of 3 horses	00	03	00
for a Veale to Hardwicke	01	06	08
&for 2 horses	00	02	00
To the overseers of the Poore Fra: Browne Hen: Booth of Mr Websters rent	05	00	00
To Job Brundley for the new Acts of the last Session	00	04	06
To the Towne Clerke for juging these accounts	00	03	04

Paid to Widd:Stringfellow which was allowed her	00	10	00
out of the Corporacon Stock to make up the interest of 200^{li} lords money 10^{li}	01	00	00
Paid Mr Coope by order of the Corporacon	05	00	00
	101	17	02

Arreares of the yeare 1678

Tho: Rollenson for 1^{li} lords money	00	01	00
John White	00	05	00
Thomas Raynor for 10^{li}	00	10	00
George Slater for 5^{li}	00	05	00
Gilbert Webster for Tho: Potts 10^{li}	00	10	00
Mr Richard Clarke Mayor for Cockpit yard	02	12	00
Edward Needham for Horse Mill and Cockpit yard	02	00	00
	06	03	00

remaines then in the Chamberlaines handes	60	12	05
paid of it to the next Chamberlaines	57	12	03
Mr Clarke debtor formerly for the horse Mill	06	00	00
for the new bible	03	00	00
for Cockpitt yard	02	12	00
for an Assize extraordinary	00	10	00
goeing to my Ld duke	00	10	00

Appendix B

Transcribed from Chesterfield Manor Court Book 1763–1841, Derbyshire Record Office, Pashley Collection, D267.

Manor and Borough of Chesterfield

The Court Leet and Great Court Baron of the Most Noble William Henry Cavendish Duke of Portland held at Chesterfield for the Manor and Borough aforesaid by the free Inquest of the Burgesses of the said Borough the twenty fifth day of October in the year of our Lord One thousand seven hundred and eighty seven Before William Manley Gentleman Deputy Steward there.

The names of the Jury Sworn

John Bale Esquire Foreman
Mr Mark Hewitt
Mr Richard Alsop
Mr Gylbert Bluett
Mr Joseph Hinde
Mr John Inman
Mr William Wingfield

Mr Thomas Brown
Mr Samuel Thacker
Mr Joseph Thacker
Mr John Barber
Mr Joseph Graham
Mr Anthony Johnson

	£	s	d
First We the Jury above named do amerce every Duke, Earl, Lord, Baronet and other Gentleman owing suit and Service to the Court and not appearing for himself or being essoigned for and not being a Burgess of this Borough		1	0
Also we amerce every Freeholder and other Inhabitant owing suit and Service to this Court and not answering for himself or being essoigned for and not being a Burgess of this Borough			4
Also we amerce every Burgess of this Borough owing Suit and Service to this Court and not answering for himself or being essoigned for			2
Also We lay a pain that if any Freeholder within the Manor and Borough aforesaid shall convey or cause to be conveyed any corn or Cattle though his Back Yard to defraud the Lord of the said Manor of his Just Toll he shall forfeit to the said Lord for such Offence		3	4
Also We lay a pain upon every Person who shall carry or suffer to be carried any Fire thro' the Streets within the Boundaries of the Manor and Borough aforesaid uncovered or shall carry or suffer to be carried any lighted Candles (Except in a Lanthorn) up and down any Yard where Straw is near that any Person so offending shall forfeit to the said Lord for every such Offence		3	4
Also We lay a pain that if any Person shall bring any Corn into the Borough aforesaid and not bring it to the Market Stones there where such Corn is to be Sold he shall forfeit to the Lord for every such Offence		3	4
Also A pain laid that if any Baker or other Person shall lay any Goss or Rammell in the Street within the Manor and Borough aforesaid within forty Yards of their own or any other House provided it be stacked or lay more than three days he shall forfeit to the said Lord for every such Offence		3	4
Also A pain laid that if any Person shall cast any dead Carcase or other carrion into the Rivers or lay the same in any Highways within the Manor and Borough aforesaid and not cover the same a sufficient depth in the Earth he shall forfeit to the said Lord for every such Offence		5	0
Also A pain laid that if any Person shall suffer any Swine to go unwrung or unyoked in the Highways or in any Street of the Manor and Borough aforesaid he shall forfeit to the said Lord for every such Offence		3	4
Also A Pain laid that if any Cellar holes or sluices be left uncovered in the Manor and Borough aforesaid the Person or Persons to whom the same shall belong shall forfeit to the said Lord for every such Offence		3	4
Also a pain laid upon every Person within the Manor and Borough aforesaid who for want of a Horse Way into their yard is forced to bring any Dung or Manure into the Streets of the said Borough that he remove it in the same day after it is laid there otherwise forfeit to the said Lord for every such Offence		3	4
Also a pain is laid that if any Person buys any Butter to sell again to forestall the Market he or she shall forfeit to the said Lord for every such Offence		3	4
Also A pain laid that if any Butcher shall Sweep or cause to be Swept any Guts Blood or Filth out of the Shambles into the			

Market Place or other Street within the Borough aforesaid he shall forfeit to the said Lord for every such Offence		3	4
Also A pain laid that if any Butcher kills any Bull within the Manor aforesaid without baiting him half an hour having a Rope and Collar for fetching he shall forfeit to the said Lord for every such Offence		3	4
Also a pain laid that if any Person shall suffer any Swine Ass or Mule to go abroad into any Street of the said Borough he shall forfeit to the Pindar two pence and to the Bailiff One penny for every such Offence			3
Also a pain laid upon every Person whomsoever living within the said Manor who shall bring and lay or cause to be brought and laid any Stones Dung Ashes or Dirt or other Rubbish whatsoever or sett any empty Hogsheads or Casks in any of the said Streets or Highways of the said Borough and shall suffer the same to be or continue to be there for upwards of six Days together so as to be a Nuisance to the Inhabitants such a Person so offending shall forfeit to the said Lord for every such Offence		3	4
Also A pain laid that if any Person within the Borough aforesaid shall after six days Notice to be given him of his Pain, suffer his Bull Dog or Mastiff to go unmuzzled within the Borough aforesaid he shall forfeit to the said Lord for every such Offence	1	0	0
Also A pain laid that if any Person within the Manor and Borough aforesaid shall lay or cause to be laid any Timber or Wood within the Market Place or within any of the Streets of the said Borough and permit the same to continue there for the space of three days he shall forfeit to the said Lord for every such Offence		3	4
Also we present Samuel Mettam (sworn) and Brailsford Hill (sworn) to be Constables and Samuel Watts (sworn) and Francis Higgins (sworn) Assistants to the Constables for the year ensuing			
Also We amerce Mr Thomas Bennett for laying or causing to be laid Rubbish in the Street before his House and permitting the same to be there for upwards of six Days so as to be a Nuisance to the Inhabitants contrary to a pain laid at the last Court the Sum of		3	4
Also We lay a pain upon Mr William Manley that if he does not effectually Secure the Roofs of his Houses in the West Barrs now uninhabited so as to prevent the same from being dangerous to Passengers by falling of Slates or otherways within 14 Days after Notice given he shall forfeit and pay to the said Lord the Sum of		3	4
Also We lay a pain upon Mr William Wingfield that if he does not effectually Secure the Roof of his House in his own Occupation in the Shambles so as to prevent the same from being dangerous to Passengers by falling of Slates or otherways within 14 days after Notice given he shall forfeit and pay to the said Lord		3	4
Also We lay a pain upon Mr Richard Parker and Mr Joseph Graham that if they do not Secure the Roofs of their Shops in the Possession of Benjamin Ling and Thomas Harvey in the Shambles so as to prevent the same from being Dangerous to Passengers by falling of Slates or otherways within 14			

days after Notice given to them respectively for that purpose each of them shall respectively forfeit and pay to the said Lord the Sum of 3 4

Also We lay a pain upon Robert Nall that if he does not Secure the Roof of his Shop in his own Possession in the Shambles so as to prevent the same from being Dangerous to Passengers by falling of Slates or otherways within 14 Days after Noticc givcn hc shall forfeit and pay to the said Lord the Sum of 3 4

Also We lay a pain upon Mr Thomas Mawkes Mr John Brown Apothecary and Mr Bernard Lucas Jun[r] that if they do not recpectively and effectually repair their respective Chimneys in their respective Dwelling Houses in Chesterfield in their respective Possessions so as to prevent the same from falling and being Dangerous to Passengers and from Fire within fourteen Days after Notice given to them respectively for that Purpose that each of them so offending shall respectively forfeit to the said Lord the Sum of 3 4

NOTES AND REFERENCES

CHAPTER 1

1. "Extracts from the common-place book of Edward Browne", *The Reliquary*-XI (1890–1), 73–8. This book of the son of Sir Thomas Browne author of *Religio Medici* is Ms 1900 in the Sloane Collection in the British Library.
2. *Journal of the Derbyshire Archaeological Society (D.A.J.),* I (1879).
3. Christopher Morris(ed), *The Journeys of Celia Fiennes,*(London, 1949), 96
4. Daniel Defoe, *A Tour through England and Wales,* (Everyman Edition 1948) II, 180.
5. B.Cozens-Hardy(ed.),*The Diary of Sylas Neville* 1767–1788 (O.U.P.,1950), 277.
6. C.B. Andrews (ed.), *The Torrington Diaries: a selection from the tours of the Hon. John Byng between the years 1781 and 1794* (1954), 172.
7. D.P. Davies, *View of Derbyshire* (1811) 550–3.
8. Richard Phillips, *A Picture of England* (1828), 231.
9. D.G. Edwards (ed.), *Derbyshire Hearth Tax Assessments 1662–70,* Derbyshire Record Society VII (1982).
10. William Salt Library, Stafford, SMS 33.
11. D.G. Edwards, "Population in Derbyshire in the reign of King Charles II: the use of hearth tax assessments and the Compton Census", *D.A.J.*, CII (1982), 106–117.
12. Sir Francis Eden, *The State of the Poor,* Vol.II (1797).
13. J. Pilkington, A View of the Present State of Derbyshire (1789).
14. Eden, *op.cit.*
15. Derbyshire Record Office (DRO), D643/A/PI 1–9.

CHAPTER 2

1. Chesterfield Public Library (CPL), Godfrey notebooks, Vol.14,120.
2. Sheffield City Libraries (SCL),Swift MSS, 1353: W. Jacques, "Gilds and Corporation Insignia", *D.A.J.,* XLIII (1921), 71–8.
3. DRO, D267, C7.
4. *Derbyshire Times,* 8 Nov.1935, "Links with the past" quotes a letter from Welbeck 18 July 1688.
5. DRO, D1622, Corporation minute books 1783–1806, 1818–1834. This section is based almost entirely on these volumes which came to light only in 1976.
6. DRO, D267, C6.
7. Chesterfield Borough Records, Chesterfield Town Hall, Clerk's Department Strongroom, Box 25.

8. *Ibid.*
9. J.C. Cox, *Three Centuries of Derbyshire Annals,* II, 21.
10. *Ibid,*II, 33.
11. Bagshaw, *Directory of Derbyshire* (1846).
12. As 7–8.
13. DRO, D267 and D1622.
14. Cited in J.M. Bestall's notes.
15. DRO, D1622.
16. *Ibid.*
17. *Ibid.*
18. *Ibid.*
19. Chesterfield Parish Church, Vestry minute books 1782–1943 (2 vols.).
20. DRO, D643/A/PO 1–4.
21. Copy of Hasland map in DRO (2048A/PO 1): Chesterfield map in the possession of Chesterfield Borough Council.
22. Eden, *op.cit.*
23. DRO, QAGr 242.
24. Report of Commissioners Enquiring into Charities, 1839: Bagshaw, *op.cit.* : DRO, D267,C6.
25. DRO, D267, A67 and C26.
26. DRO, D267, A67.
27. DRO, D267, Chesterfield Manor Court book 1763–1841 J.M. Bestall, "The Court Leet and Great Court Baron of Chesterfield 1763–1841", *D.A.J.,*LXX-VI (1956),27–33.

CHAPTER 3

1. DRO, Quarter Sessions records, land tax assessments: DRO,D63.
2. DRO, D63.
3. Few of the original records of these trading companies have been traced – only the regulations of the Company of Mercers in the Blockley papers (DRO, D1622) have so far come to light. This account of the trading companies is therefore based largely on a note in the Swift MSS (SCL, Swift MSS, 1353) and on the extracts from the orders of the three companies printed in J. Walton, *Chesterfield Almanack and Tradesmens Advertiser for 1868.* They were summarised by W. Jacques in "Gilds and corporation Insignia", *D.A.J.,* XLIII (1921), 73–6.
4. SCL, Swift MSS, 1353.
5. Richard Blome, Britannia (1673), 77–8.
6. C. Kerry, "Leonard Wheatcroft of Ashover", *D.A.J,*XVIII (1896), 29–80: C. Kerry, "The Autobiography of Leonard Wheatcroft, *D.A.J.* XXI (1899), 26–55.
7. Nottinghamshire Record Office (NRO), DD.P.60/25–7.
8. G.G. Hopkinson, "The development of inland navigation in South Yorkshire and North Derbyshire 1697–1850", *Transactions of the Hunter Archaeological Society,*VII(1956), 229–51: T.S. Willan, *The early history of the Don Navigation*(1965), 63,99,152.
9. Willan, *op.cit.,* 6–7, 74, 152, 156.
10. Willan, *op.cit.,*7.
11. DRO, D267, C3.
12. *Bailey's Western and Midland Directory or Merchants and Tradesmans Useful Companion for the year 1783.*
13. Pilkington, *op.cit.,*338–9.

14. DRO, D643/A/PW 44.
15. DRO, land tax assessments.
16. *Ibid.*
17. *Ibid.*
18. *Pigot's Commercial Directory of Derbyshire,* 1835, reprint by Derbyshire County Library 1976.
19. Largely based on Philip Robinson, *The Smiths of Chesterfield* (1957).
20. J. Farey, "*General View of the Agriculture and Minerals of Derbyshire* (1811), I, 397.
21. H.R. Johnson and A.W. Skempton, "*William Strutt's cotton mills* 1793–1812", *Transactions of the Newcomen Society,* XXX(1956), 179–205 and "The first iron frames", *Architectural Review,*March 1962, 175–186.
22. SCL, S(heffield) S(melting) C(ompany) 76.
23. Richard Phillips,*A picture of England*(1828), 232–238.

CHAPTER 4

1. Most recently J.C.V. Kendall and M.P. Jackson, *A History of the Free Grammar School Chesterfield* (1965).
2. CPL, Handford Collection, Box.5.
3. DRO, D267, C44.
4. CPL, Handford Collection, Box 5.
5. *Ibid.*
6. Kendall and Jackson, *op.cit.*,8.
7. *Ibid.*,9.
8. DRO, D1622, Borough minutes.
9. *Ibid.*
10. *Ibid.*,26.9.1803.
11. *Ibid.*,8.4.1804.
12. *Ibid.*,18.3.1822.
13. *Ibid.*, 19.3.1823.
14. *Ibid.*,18.6.1823.
15. *Ibid.*,23.9.1823.
16. M.R.Austin, *The Church in Derbyshire 1823–4,*Derbyshire Record Series 5 (1974), entry for Chesterfield, 61–62.
17. DRO, D1622, Borough minutes, 23.9.1829.
18. J.M. Bestall (ed.D.V. Fowkes), *History of Chesterfield, Vol.III, Early Victorian Chesterfield,* Chapter 9.
19. Abstract of the Answers and Returns relating to the Number of Schools, and the Particulars thereof, in each Town, Parish, Chapelry etc. in England and Wales(Bedford to Lancaster volume). House of Lords Sessional Papers 1835, xxxi. Chesterfield entry on p.146.
20. DRO, D267, B47.

CHAPTER 5

1. Douglas W. Robson, *The Story of the Elder Yard Unitarian Chapel* (revised by Arthur Vallance in 1967).
2. CPL, Godfrey notebooks, transcript of glebe terrier 1693.
3. Lichfield Joint Record Office, B/C/5 Probate records.
4. *Transactions of the Hunter Archaeological Society,*Vol.IV pt.1(1929–30), 79.
5. *Alum.Cant.*, I,161.
6. *Alum.Cant.*,I,57.
7. J.C.Cox, "Chesterfield church customs of the eighteenth century", *D.A.J.*, XII(1890),162–9.

8. DRO, D267, C29.
9. College of Arms, Pegge MSS II, 131, 299.
10. *Ibid.*
11. DRO, D267, C34.
12. College of Arms, Pegge MSS II, 121–3.
13. At the time Chesterfield parish records were surveyed in 1970 these accounts were not found. Their present whereabouts is not known.
14. DRO, D267, C11.
15. CPL. file P8, X1491.
16. M.R. Austin, *op.cit.,* 61–2.
17. DRO, Quarter Sessions records.
18. William Salt Library, Stafford, SMS 33.
19. "The life of Master John Shaw" in *Yorkshire Diaries,* Surtees Society LXV (1877), 119–162, also appendix for sermons and other writings 358–444, particularly 433–5.
20. William Wainwright a curate at the parish church with the vicar Matthew Waddington, who was censured in the 1636/7 visitation for failure to wear a surplice and to administer communion.
21. Samuel Palmer, *The Nonconformist Memorial* (1775),I,208.
22. Robson and Vallance, *op.cit.,* 5.
23. Palmer, *op.cit.,* I, 315.
24. George Fox, *Journal of George Fox*(Everyman), 30–34.
25. Much of this account of the development of Quakerism in the Chesterfield area is based on an unpublished account of early Quakerism in the Chesterfield area, by H.Le Noury.
26. *The Journal of the Life of that Ancient Servant of Christ, John Gratton,* (London, 1720). A brief account is given in J.C. Cox, *Three Centuries of Derbyshire Annals,* I, 341–5.
27. Unpublished thesis, D. Roberts, "The History of Quakerism in Derbyshire". (Copy in CPL).
28. Cox, *op.cit.,*346.
29. Alan Cole, "The Quakers and the English Revolution", *Past and Present,* 10(1956), 39–54.
30. DRO, Q/RI/98.
31. Cox,*op.cit.,* I, 367.
32. DRO, Quarter Sessions records.
33. As 25.
34. Robson and Vallance, *op.cit.*
35. S.C.Newton, "The gentry of Derbyshire in the 17th century", *D.A.J.,*LXXXVI(1966), 15–6.
36. The Elder Yard Chapel deeds and related documents are deposited in Chesterfield Public Library: also abstract of conveyance to trustees in DRO, D267, C146.
37. T.Ford, *A History of Chesterfield,* 133.
38. E.D.Heathcote, *The family of Heathcote*(1899), 57.
39. Cox,*op.cit.,*I, 362 (Ogle), 364(Ferne), 365(Bagshawe), 367–8 (List of registered meeting houses).
40. W.H.G.Bagshawe, *The Bagshawes of Ford* (1886), 8(ordination),26(Ashford).
41. I am indebted to Mr.W.Watkinson for this account of the origins of Methodism in Chesterfield.
42. Ford, *op.cit.*

BIBLIOGRAPHY

C.B.Andrews(ed.), *The Torrington Diaries: a selection from the tours of the Hon.John Byng between the years 1781 and 1794* (1954).

M.R. Austin, *The church in Derbyshire 1823–4,* Derbyshire Record Series 5 (1974).

J. Bagshaw, *Directory of Derbyshire* (1846).

Bailey's Western and Midland Directory or Merchants and Tradesmans Useful Companion for the year 1783.

J.M.Bestall (ed.D.V.Fowkes), *History of Chesterfield, Vol.III, Early Victorian Chesterfield* (1978).

J.C.Cox, *Three Centuries of Derbyshire Annals* (1890)

B.Cozens-Hardy (ed.), *The Diary of Sylas Neville 1767–1788* (O.U.P., 1950).

D.P.Davies, *View of Derbyshire* (1811)

Daniel Defoe, *A Tour through England and Wales* (Everyman Edition 1948).

Sir Francis Eden, *The State of the Poor* (1797).

D.G.Edwards (ed.), *Derbyshire Hearth Tax Assessments 1662–1670,* Derbyshire Record Society VII (1982).

J. Farey, *General View of the Agriculture and Minerals of Derbyshire.*(1811).

T.Ford, *A History of Chesterfield* (1839).

J. Glover, *Directory of Derbyshire* (1829).

E.D.Heathcote, *The family of Heathcote* (1899).

J.C.V. Kendall and M.P. Jackson, *A History of the Free Grammar School Chesterfield* (1965).

Christopher Morris (ed.), *The Journeys of Celia Fiennes* (London 1949).

Sir Richard Phillips, *A Picture of England* (1828).

Pigot's Commercial Directory of Derbyshire 1835 (reprint by Derbyshire Library Service 1976).

J. Pilkington, *A View of the Present State of Derbyshire* (1789).

Philip Robinson, *The Smiths of Chesterfield* (1957).
D.W.Robson, *The Story of the Elder Yard Unitarian Chapel* (revised by A. Vallance, 1967).
T.S.Willan, *The early history of the Don Navigation* (1965).

INDEX

HISTORY OF CHESTERFIELD

1 **Early and Medieval Chesterfield.** By J.M. Bestall. Pp. viii + 176. 1974. £3.50.

2:1 **Tudor and Stuart Chesterfield.** By Philip Riden. Pp. xvi + 240. 1984. £5.00.

2:2 **Restoration and Georgian Chesterfield.** By J.M. Bestall and D.V. Fowkes. Pp. xxx + 000. 1984. £3.50.

3 **Early Victorian Chesterfield.** By J.M. Bestall (Edited by D.V. Fowkes). Pp. xii + 140. 1978. £5.00.

5 **Records of the Borough of Chesterfield and related documents, 1204–1835.** Edited by Philip Riden and John Blair. Pp. xx + 316. 1980. £15.00

Volume four will complete the series

Available from booksellers or from the Chief Financial Officer, Town Hall, Chesterfield S40 1LP